Assessment Tools and Systems

Assessment Tools and Systems

Meaningful Feedback Approaches to Promote Critical and Creative Thinking

Barbara J. Smith

ROWMAN & LITTLEFIELD
Lanham • Boulder • New York • London

Published by Rowman & Littlefield
An imprint of The Rowman & Littlefield Publishing Group, Inc.
4501 Forbes Boulevard, Suite 200, Lanham, Maryland 20706
www.rowman.com

86-90 Paul Street, London EC2A 4NE, United Kingdom

Copyright © 2022 by Barbara J. Smith

All rights reserved. No part of this book may be reproduced in any form or by any electronic or mechanical means, including information storage and retrieval systems, without written permission from the publisher, except by a reviewer who may quote passages in a review.

British Library Cataloguing in Publication Information Available

Library of Congress Cataloging-in-Publication Data

Names: Smith, Barbara J., 1956- author.
Title: Assessment tools and systems : meaningful feedback approaches to promote critical and creative thinking / Barbara J. Smith.
Description: Lanham : Rowman & Littlefield, [2022] | Includes bibliographical references. | Summary: "This book was written to acknowledge the key role quality assessment can play in engaging all school community members in critical and creative thinking"—Provided by publisher.
Identifiers: LCCN 2022019144 (print) | LCCN 2022019145 (ebook) | ISBN 9781475867688 (cloth) | ISBN 9781475867695 (paperback) | ISBN 9781475867701 (epub)
Subjects: LCSH: Educational tests and measurements. | Educational change. | School improvement programs. | Feedback (Psychology)
Classification: LCC LB3051 .S566 2022 (print) | LCC LB3051 (ebook) | DDC 371.26–dc23/eng/20220803
LC record available at https://lccn.loc.gov/2022019144
LC ebook record available at https://lccn.loc.gov/2022019145

*Dedicated to my family.
In my first year of retirement Simon,
Sarah, Martin & Molly
who endure my hope, obsession
and quest for an ideal education.
Thank you for the gift of family
when the world is getting to be more complicated every day.*

Contents

Acknowledgments	ix
Introduction . . . A Dog's Breakfast	xi
1: Look Up: What If?	1
2: Truncated Testing: What If?	7
3: Reporting Reform: What If?	25
4: Classroom Grading: What If?	39
5: Assessment of Portfolios, Experiential Learning, and Awarding Micro-credentials: What If?	51
6: Top Dog: What If?	63
7: Underdogs: What If?	67
8: Cycles of Teacher Feedback, Performance Reviews, and Professional Growth: What If?	75
9: Growth of School Leaders and Teacher-Leaders: What If . . .	101
10: Growth of Non-Instructional Staff: What If . . .	111
11: Who Assesses the Watch Dogs?: Why If?	117
12: Goodwill Hunting: What If?	121
13: School Assessment Whisperers: What If?	127
14: The Sound of Silence: What If?	135
15: Forging New Paths for School Assessment	141
References	147

Acknowledgments

There are many experts, role models, family, and friends I would like to thank for their inspiration. To everyone who pens a comment, a document, an article, or a book about improving assessment in schools, I say thank you for speaking up, and motivating me to add one more fuel cell to the rushing roar of testing dissatisfaction. Every day I was ready to send in this manuscript, another dozen articles burst on the screen. To honor all the ideas and legacies of these writers would require an encyclopedia format to address all works saved in my seemingly never-ending assessment folder.

I'd like to acknowledge the folks who took time to read the beginnings of this skeleton manuscript of *Assessment Tools and Systems: Meaningful Feedback Approaches to Promote Critical and Creative Thinking*. The ideas shared and questions posed helped to further shape this work. Many thanks to Kevin Bartlett, Jackie Delong, Pat Diamond, Michael Fullan, Judith Green, Wayne Jones, Bena Kallick, Cheryl Lacey, Mike Lawrence, Kris Machtmes, Sheryl MacMath, Douglas Reeves, Ted Spear, Larry Swartz, and Mark Williams. Many thanks to all reviewers and experts dedicated to assessment reform.

I continue to be inspired by exceptional educators and leaders. Madelaine Allan, Lauren Black, Mike Carter, Terence Carter, Tanisha Nugent Chang, Denise Cherry, Bob Chilton, Jim Christopher, Luke Coles, Jackie Copp, Stevonna Cordova, Mike Crowley, Susan Drake, Radu Elias, Rosemary Evans, Alan Ginsburg, Audrey LeVault, Ashley Lopez, Lisa Gonzales, Craig Griffie, Mhairi Johnson, Dennis Kellison, Deanna Kensler, Diane Manica, Marion McKeiver, Jack Miller, Talithia Palmer, Shaune Palmer, Martha Perry, Skip Phoenix, Angela Purcell, Valerie Rixon, Mary Robbins, Ian Robinson, Jalen Rose, Michelle Ruscitti-Miller, Keith Russell, Anne Shaw, Brian Stone, Toby Travis, Valerie Turner, Tony Upson, Emily Walton-Doris, Kamilla Wheeler, William Williams, Anne Wintemute, Rick Wormeli, and, posthumously, David Booth, Don Fawcett, Wayne Sommerville, Dave Stevenson, and Kirk Wipper. I want to add a special recognition for my OISE mentees, Babak Bagheri and Emily Beaton. Change takes time but a mighty thanks is earned by those with boots on the ground. With such commitment to positive change in schools, fortune should favor the brave!

All who edit books are masters of removing distractions, so I am truly appreciative of all who contributed their keen eyes to this work, namely, Wayne Jones, Beverly Scudamore, and the publisher and the editorial team at Rowman & Littlefield. Many thanks to Acquisitions Editor Tom Koerner; who guided me to make some fierce revisions; Assistant Editor Kira Hall; Managing Editor Carlie Wall, for all her support in coordinating and detailing this project; and Production Editor Megan DeLancey.

For decades, I have escaped cooking and other domestic duties to be an educator and author, so my partner, Simon, should be knighted for the key role he plays in supporting me and my schooling pursuits. His work in the oil industry provided many opportunities for me to explore so many different kinds of educational institutions as an expatriate and educator at home and abroad. Daughter Sarah continues to inspire, breaking through gender barriers selling heavy equipment for Hilti Corporation. I equally admire my son Martin's drive and capacity for investment banking at Jefferies Financial Group in New York. My hard-working daughter-in-law, Molly Nelson, attends to details daily as a lawyer in Manhattan. Our rescue dog, Blossom from Louisiana, brings much joy and keeps me walking 4km every morning. Blossom follows a lineage of four-legged family members including Mickey and Flossie, who collectively contributed to the peppering of the assessment tails/tales that wag too many schools today.

Finally, I must apologize to readers who may not be familiar with the penned pockets of pop culture embedded within this book. I am a shameless lover of all things that spark ingenuity (science fiction, fantasy), inspire hope, and embrace change. Programs like the *Outer Limits*, *Star Trek,* or *Game of Thrones* have all dabbled with my imagination. I grew up watching Captain Kirk and Engineer Scottie solve insurmountable problems. Not only did I view each episode of *Star Trek*, I also purchased my own USS Enterprise uniform. Apart from writing a few more books, my bucket list includes being a delegate at a *Star Trek* convention, as Gene Roddenberry (*Star Trek* creator) and I share the same birthdate!

Introduction . . . A Dog's Breakfast

In the test tube of life, we encounter an extensive menu of options for assessing the value of work, so many you might consider it a dog's breakfast. How can we assess and hold students, teachers, administrators, trustees, and school systems accountable for contributing to a quality education? Furthermore, how can we determine which assessment tools and processes are more effective than others?

While there are high expectations particularly for students in school, it is rare for a stakeholder to examine or challenge the quality of assessment tools, as well as their timing, volume, and purpose. Many schools simply go about implementing a monotonous mediocre meal of assessment practices as directed. Such incessant testing experiences, in concert with less than adequate student engagement levels, have thrust schools into a scrambled existence.

Fast forward into the new blended teaching and learning world brought on by the recent pandemic. The school community must now exist in a digital interface like never before. The advent of COVID-19 has turned schools upside down; educators have not faced such rapid change. With the newfound complexities, it is possible to become overly optimistic about returning to a perceived "simple" normal, the space everyone is accustomed to, whether it was a healthy meal or not.

On the one hand, the pandemic has served as a serious distraction, interfering with the path of innovation and school improvment; on the other hand, it can function as a stimulus to disrupt the wave of "sameness" in schools. Rather than focusing on implementing testing systems that were never hitting the mark for every student, it is time to refresh the waves of curriculum and testing with a mandate to transform ineffective assessment encounters.

Schools need to bring on more meaningful and constructive feedback practices to support an industrious and sustainable future. There are plenty of policies in schools today that are dedicated to determining the quality of student work, yet have you ever wondered if there are quality controls of the assessments used to evaluate students, teachers, and other school-related community members?

Should educators just accept assessment tools or approaches as they currently exist, as a rite of passage or a necessary hurdle? Should teachers not seek to understand how tests are designed or if the results are truly reliable? If everything else in the world can improve via change, then assessment systems can evolve, too.

What if all school community members knew more about assessment? What if quality feedback was something all students could embrace? What if all school employees experienced growth in concert with quality feedback and performance appraisals? To move from some to all, or most, is a significant goal for improving current assessment practices in schools. Before shifting to new forms of assessment, it's important to take stock of existing flaws before we can seriously consider other possibilities.

All that happens in the teaching and learning culture of the classroom can never be captured on a single test or an assignment. Most assessment tools present only partial evidence of learning. By examining the limitations of assessment, educators can learn how to adjust and improve feedback tools and systems in ways that can further enhance teaching and learning.

Students, teachers, workers, TV shows, movies, music, and a plethora of consumer products that tempt potential procurements are assessed one way or another. Some may be both excited and numb by the five-star ratings, the "Blue Ribbon" award winners, the SAT scores, the Olympic Gold Medals, the Billboard charts, and even *Oprah's Book Club* picks. But do most people trust how such determinations and selections are made?

Sports fans can be glued to screens to find out who will win the Super Bowl, the World Series, the NBA Championship, or the Stanley Cup; for the most part, the team with the highest score wins—pretty straight forward, right? Yet, the selection of a Rhodes Scholar or a Nobel Peace Prize recipient is not necessarily so clear.

While it is easy to see the influence of subjectivity and popularity in award selection, many may not be aware of the biased nature of testing in schools. With so much riding on grades and test scores, it is surprising that more helicopter parents have not circled their wagons around the nature of the assessment tools themselves.

Many parents may question how the tools are interpreted, but rarely do they issue a challenge about the quality of the tool itself. School systems seemingly benefit the privileged few. There is often a resistance to any change that could thwart the same path to school success that worked for them. Those fortunate enough to benefit from assessment practices want to ensure the same opportunities continue for their children and grandchildren. Making changes to the system to increase opportunities for more students can be perceived by the privileged few as deliberately attacking their experienced route to success in school.

The textbook and test-making industries have much to gain by maintaining the status quo. It can be a lucrative business counting on a human thirst for ranking. An abundance of slick glossy binders and prefabricated test kits are readily available for all who assume that high stakes testing is the most effective measure of potential talent and intelligence.

Even though the research does not support such a claim, this is the fake news that is perpetuated, and not challenged particularly by political forces in education. At what point will all decision-makers in education address the question: Is the purpose of school to support teaching and learning or the testing industry?

It matters that schools nurture and develop the talent and capacity of our young people. After all, they will be the solvers of tomorrow's problems, struggles so serious that they can challenge humanity's very existence. So yes, tools that serve as barometers of intelligence and talent can and do matter. However, we cannot pretend they are foolproof indicators of absolute learning. An educated society should recognize that assessment tools and feedback systems need to evolve in order to serve the needs of a changing world.

This book is written for both the consumers of assessment and the designers of the tools used to provide feedback and evaluate performance in schools. Throughout our lives, we are tested in ways that appear to be highly sophisticated and functional, however, many tools used for the purpose of judging and ranking can be highly subjective and ineffective. Many educators willingly accept the results of testing data, assuming that the test designs are sound, not considering that dependable assessment tools can be a rare find.

Educators and leaders in schools and universities often trust the content of tests, which when consumed can lead to the collection of arbitrary data and questionable interpretations of what the results can mean. Depending on the magnitude of the response, the assumption that any test result is an absolute indicator of learning can have serious implications; a simplification of findings can lead to the closing of schools and lost dreams. School systems can do better.

Most people have experienced tests in school, but rarely is much time dedicated to thinking about how well schools prepare students for taking them, and if the test questions were actually part of a curriculum that was taught. This book aims to undress how testing without careful attention to detail can make a mess of things, in other words a "dog's breakfast."

To help fashion a more engaging experience in school, educators need to unravel assumptions about assessment and testing, and consider more rigorous and impactful feedback practices. This look at ways education systems rate kids and appraise the professionals who teach them is worthy of more extensive examination.

How sure are educators and other school community members that test scores or performance reviews lead people on a capacity-building path toward their potential? Making time for a deep dive into the not so obvious world of assessment can be well worth this investment of time. When schools can identify the limitations in their gauges, they can hopefully create better tools that can help society develop young people, and the adults who guide them, to make wiser life and long-term learning choices.

Regrettably, most families have been well-conditioned at retrieving the tests thrown at them. In dog language, students know how to sit down, lie down, or roll over, on demand. Many jump through testing hoops, without really questioning their purpose.

When assessments are challenged, it is not uncommon to hear reactions such as: "Tests build character and resilience"; "Young people need to cope with the rigor of the real world"; and, "It's the only fair way to make decisions about college admissions!" Argh! And, wait for it—the lame reprise: "Nothing's going to change, anyway."

Whatever, the latest justification fueling the tolerance for testing, too many people take testing for granted. Don't most people want to take fewer tests? Don't learners want to be judged fairly? Don't students or former students care that tests may be flawed? While this book is about the tests that shape the lives inside school, it is also about paying tribute to trailblazers who tackle assessment challenges head on.

Teachers, school leaders, and university researchers working side-by-side conducting action research in the context of real classrooms have the foresight and expertise to see the connections between assessment, curriculum, teaching, and learning.

Building better ways of assessment cannot happen in isolation of school improvement. There have been many initiatives and models of collaborative action that have led to assessment transformations, the kind that support more engaged and encouraging school cultures. *Assessment Tools and Systems: Meaningful Feedback Approaches to Promote Critical and Creative Thinking* is not a meal for the "go with the flow" educator, parent, or teacher who passively accepts the current fate of testing.

While this work aims to dissect assumptions about the value of testing, it also addresses possibilities for how assessment can play a significant role in learning, not just a record of learning. On the one hand, there can be collateral damage from testing when schools and systems toy with people's lives and futures. On the other hand, when assessment and feedback are grounded in solid educational theory, the possibilities are endless. This book can be a creative and constructive place for building better feedback tools and processes, aligned with courageous goals of increasing the critical mass of an educated society.

It is time for a new school assessment story, one that minimizes and limits the potency of weak assessment practices. Perhaps riding the dark wave of ranking assessment will make it easier to recognize more constructive assessment options in the light at the end of this seemingly turbulent tunnel. At times, this message may seem like a band-aid has been ripped off a fresh wound.

This work is not a bureaucratic read, buried in mounds of jargon and prose. It registers a direct concern about the limitations of testing while proposing alternative ideas for making assessment a connected and value-added part of the curriculum.

And, for the dog lovers, the canine analogies are intended to add some humorous banter to the mix. Each chapter highlights distinct perspectives on the assessment experiment that can impact so many educated lives.

Chapter 1, "Look Up," appeals to all stakeholders to look beyond what exists as typical assessment practices today. Educators all need to learn more about assessment in schools and speak up about the need for change. In many ways, commercial test-makers can exert too much control over the school curriculum; their emphasis on ranking students mirrors their ruling on an "iron throne." These emperor voices might machinate with "don't look up . . . we've got this," but this would be a naïve assumption.

This chapter unpacks the rationale for gaining insight into these stealth-like players, the people who pay for the widgets and the salaries of testing policy-makers. This chapter urges everyone to look up and consider new ways to address more informed assessment practices.

The second chapter, "Truncated Testing," focuses on how the school community can come to understand the limitations of what many refer to as high stakes testing. This chapter examines how standardized tests are truncated, representing an extremely limited account of learning. Students, teachers, school leaders, parents, and trustees are urged to unite and question the volume and necessity of standardized testing practices.

Bystanders, who trust the system, believe that all that is needed is a subtle tweaking of the tools and implementation processes, not wide-scale disruption. The word disruption may seem unsettling, but this, with the courage of brave school leaders, is exactly what is needed to reduce any reliance on truncated data as a full representation of teaching and learning.

Chapter 3, "Reporting Reform," challenges the standardization of report cards and reporting practices, and the impact such documents and processes can have on the sameness of curriculum, void from cultural imprinting and ownership. The goal of ranking students should no longer be a priority for reporting. Students and families need to know what evidence of learning addresses what has been mastered and, therefore, can be applied in other settings.

The lack of research on effective report cards and reporting systems is surprising, given the money invested in testing and other forms of assessment. This chapter acknowledges that the school curriculum should not be separate from assessment. School improvement should include the growth and evolution of reporting practices, too.

Chapter 4, "Classroom Grading" invites teachers to the assessment table. Educators are skilled and talented professionals who are very capable of designing effective classroom assessments that contribute to learning. This chapter features the need to support teachers in their bid to develop fair and transparent assessment tools. Teachers are encouraged to examine existing tests and rubrics with an eye to using them as learning tools. Caution is advised for teachers who rely on one-size-fits-all assessment resources that are not created in the contexts of the students learning environment.

Using portfolios, making room for experiential learning, and chunking learning into micro-credentials are the focus in Chapter 5. Even the Carnegie credit should change, evolve, and improve. There is much education can learn from what engages learners outside the school system. It's time to open the K-16 doors to more innovative learning that can come from project-based learning, portfolio making, and participation in micro-credential and smaller chunked courses.

"Top Dog," Chapter 6, highlights the unrealistic high hopes of many parents who want their child to be the "top dog" in their school class. In the current system, the ranking of 25 students, means that 24 parents would have such hopes dashed. Such pipe dreams begin with echoes of proud parents lamenting report cards filled with all As. This chapter satirically muses about and questions the traditional way report cards and GPAs are developed and implemented in today's schools.

There are better ways to attract and motivate more students to focus on mastery, rather than anointing a single "top dog." Admission directors in universities are encouraged to rethink testing tools they may have previously trusted as key drivers for their acceptance decisions.

Many students are referred to as "Underdogs," which is the title of Chapter 7, because they are recipients, for the most part, of what everyone else is doing to them. These stakeholders matter; ALL students matter. While few students have a say in what happens at school, it is important to consider that they can have more opportunities to examine their own learning and assessment contexts. How often do we ask students about the quality of the rubric or testing tool that was used to assess their learning?

Students can add their voices to the mix, but the bigger dogs in the dog park need to make room for more achievers. Whether identified with special needs, or not, students who are not the "top dogs" have much to teach us about engagement and school improvement.

Chapter 8, "Cycles of Teacher Feedback, Performance Reviews, and Professional Growth," reveals flaws associated with connecting student achievement and staff performance review. This chapter emphasizes the need for clarity of feedback and performance within a fair process, one that links developing professionally as a significant part of an overall teacher's growth cycle. Having a performance review is not enough. Just as students require quality tools to support their assessment, so too do teachers.

Chapter 9 follows with a view of school leader feedback, and chapter 10 addresses the assessment and feedback for non-instructional staff in schools.

"Who Assesses the Watchdogs?" (chapter 11) features ways we can assess school leaders and political representatives; both can do much more than attend meetings and approve budgets. This chapter warns of potential repercussions of the uninformed trustee, and governance links to conflicts of interest.

As much as a great school leader is not simply a manager, a great school board should not be a sleepy one. Both can be active, engaged, and willing to give their time generously. This chapter showcases how trailblazer trustees can challenge conventional testing practices and how some are stepping up to learn more about education, not only in terms of modelling lifelong learning, but equipping themselves to make informed decisions.

Chapter 12 features a parody on "Goodwill Hunting," not the movie, but the lack of rigor employed by many nonprofit agencies acting on behalf of wealthy donors who want to park their dollars in educational charities. This chapter provides solid suggestions on how to empower philanthropists to be more informed about the possibilities for their donations, and not simply reliant on quantitative data to determine the impact of their investments.

Chapter 13, "School Assessment Whisperers," speaks about assessment and the underlying power struggles in schools. All is not as elegant as it seems in today's schools. Lots of talk comes from the head office about embracing change, but few line up to challenge testing forces fueling the Army of the Dead (the test-makers). Unfortunately, there are too many kingdoms that operate in "set in stone" cultures, keeping vigorous change from taking hold. In such schools, there are some pioneers risking whispers of new testing approaches, ideas worthy of deeper thought and action.

"The Sound of Silence," chapter 14, echoes the need for bystanders to step up and ask the tough questions about the value of testing and assessments in school.

Finally, Chapter 15, "Forging New Paths for School Assessment," is a call for public action. The purpose of this chapter is to shake things up with a bucket list of assessment ideas for the public to consider to help put schools on the cutting edge of engagement and reform. There can be more seats at the school table; the public can take part; educators can all share ideas about how testing can contribute to school improvement. More community members can support constructive change in schools.

Unlike competitive sports, schools should not be a game of winners and losers. There's no time like the present to rethink dated habits and strike out poor testing practices. Stakeholders can do this by accessing and challenging the insider workings and rules of the testing game. Educators can have a say in generating a new age playing field, where all students succeed. Tests do not have to be the weapons for determining who sits on the iron throne. How the system uses testing and gives the practice unwarranted status is where schools fail so many learners.

By taking this journey inside some rusty chambers of school assessment structures, one can begin to see how the quantity and volume of testing in North America today, is turning grapes into vinegar factories. For many people, testing does not quench one's thirst, nor does it inspire an appetite for learning. Rarely do community members get an opportunity to grapple with and think deeply about the authenticity of testing practices in schools. A more informed public could shift the tide of ignorance that feeds the "nothing can change, anyway" or "that's just the way it is" defense of the status quo.

While many experts denounce the idea of schools as testing factories (Campbell, Danielson, Darling-Hammond, Fullan, Hargreaves, O'Connor, Stiggins, Wiggins, Wormeli), it is disappointing that such challenges seem to be drowned out by demands for accountability that assume that more testing will improve learning. For the most part, expert testimony is muted and, sadly, ignored. So, the promise of this text is to thrust a curveball into the system to challenge assumptions and abuses of school assessment. The inner organs of testing are not as fair as they should be.

It was no easy feat selecting the focus for the fifteen chapters that follow. This read is a condensed collection of serious concerns about testing with a refreshing twist of new options for consideration. More importantly, this menu invites the reader to bring more testing experiences to the table. Educators should be permitted and encouraged to share in the development of an improved nutritious test plan, one that scales back the portions, significantly.

Educators no longer need a big gulp of a supersized meal to quench a thirst for testing. Testing decisions need to be rooted in a deeper understanding of growth mindsets. It matters that stakeholders are more aware of the misinformation that can fuel the overuse of standardized testing practices.

Rather than follow a conventional textbook pattern filled with chapter ending questions, this book begins each chapter with a hypothetical proposition "What if . . . ", for some initial reflection and discussion, if so moved. Then it's head first into the murky world of school testing. At the end of each chapter, Action Items are posed for consideration. Each begins with one of three verbs: pause, start, or study. Buckle up for a ride through a new black hole of assessment. The school testing experiment is about to be centrifuged, and unpacked for human consumption.

1

Look Up

What If?

WHAT IF STAKEHOLDERS TOOK MORE TIME TO LEARN ABOUT ASSESSMENT IN SCHOOLS, WHAT COULD HAPPEN?

It is time to look up and put the weapons of assessment on hold, at least until such time as this examination has addressed current research on assessment practices, and subsequently asked questions about evaluative actions in schools. Even though testing should not be the central focus of schools, it is often the hard heel that drives what and how students learn. Teachers, students, and parents are expected to accept the prognosis of various assessments that arise out of random and one-size-fits-all approaches to teaching and learning.

The echo "don't look up" looms large in schools following the testing code. The message that test-takers keep their heads down, with eyes focused squarely on the test, is profound. And, educators can only expand assessment options when they are permitted to look up and identify alternatives. There can be more options than what are promoted by the dominant forces that support the narrow focus on standardized testing, prevalent in so many US charter schools today.

Referring to a failed system of education, Lee (2019) passionately registered his concern that everyday schooling, for too many, is more about doing damage to the least number of students[1] rather than doing things differently to reach them all. Educators can be so caught up in the fine-tuning of testing practices, that there is little time left to inspire and teach. It takes courage to question testing practices and an overcrowded curriculum.

There are educators who swim against the testing tide, and there are others who let the assessment tail wag the dog. Like the driver who ignores ominous clanking sounds coming from a car, seemingly forecasting eminent danger, it can be easy to ignore the warning sounds of a broken assessment system. "Turning up the music," is one way to avoid dealing with a probable car repair, but a short-term reprieve will not make the problem disappear.

In many ways, turning a blind eye to the value of testing is how educators and parents turn up the volume to avoid addressing serious assessment flaws in many education systems. Test-makers can be masters of the art of making the simple complex. While countless hours go into the crafting of tests, the hard work cannot excuse the integrating of masking and cloaking options for student test item selection. The goal should not be to trick a large proportion of the test-takers. Such regressive actions, are more focused on what students do not know, rather than what they do.

Standardized scores function to spread students out on a normative curve; such distributive scores can make it easier for admission teams to make decisions about who is the best fit for their schools. For far too long many public and educational experts have simply turned up the music, rather than challenging assumptions that an arbitrary bell curve should spit out determinations about who can belong in what programs at what schools.

The test-making industry seems to be disconnected to the research on informed practices in teaching and learning and curriculum design. What motivates the test-makers who simplify an education to selected items from multiple choice tests? Some may believe that the results reveal widespread strength or weakness in a school or school district. Many, however, may see the adoption of standardized testing and practice testing as a lucrative way to feast on the public trough.

In the United States, many test designers are publishing companies, who have much to gain when schools, desperate for needing high scores, not only purchase the practice tests, but all the textbook series they promote, as well. In more civil places, the test-makers at least work for universities who have less to gain from taking on test construction projects.

Many test-makers wield significant power as they place considerable faith in the precision of flawed tools. Unlike the chefs who control testing recipes and ingredients, the test-takers, do not have a menu of choice. It's the same meal for everyone, and if a student needs alternative ways to demonstrate their understanding, that's not considered by many as an equitable component of a standardized test.

Often standardized test implementors suggest that the results are only a slice of learning, which indeed they are, but how such scores are weighted does not tend to be aligned with informed practices on differentiation and individualization. How can school systems address the dichotomy that arises from trust in standardization at the same time purporting that one size of teaching does not fit all learners?

During the first two years of COVID-19, there were some jurisdictions that put a hold on standardized tests for a variety of reasons. The idea that such results could not be attained from a single sanitary classroom setting aroused concerns that students could be in an easier position to cheat. Others were concerned that a mix of lockdown and face-to-face teaching was not conducive for testing in a fair playing field. During this time, teaching and learning took precedence over tests that were cancelled.

It could be argued that any learning loss during this chaotic time had more to do with students not being in a classroom, not that they missed out on a standardized test. Finally, there was agreement that economic disparity made it impossible to ensure that all students had equal access to resources to help them learn in their varied home environments. The pandemic brought to everyone's attention that not every child has access to a computer or technology, and that, pandemic or not, such a variable impacts results on standardized tests.

In many schools COVID-19 helped put standardized testing in perspective. Teachers did their best to teach online, or from the end of a driveway; they were free and permitted to teach beyond the test. COVID-19 did bring to the forefront the contrast between the haves and the have-nots, but it also shed light on the value of teacher and classroom feedback and assessment.

During the COVID pandemic ranking and comparing results did not take precedence over the individualized needs of each student. Teachers could focus on 21st-century skill development[2]; they could determine what was essential to support deep learning, the kind that gives students experiences that can enhance their capacity to make significant contributions in college, work, and life.

In a standardized testing-focused world, it's okay for students to have their own learning meal, as long as everyone can be subjected to the same standardized assessment at the same time, assuming all students of the same age should be at the same place at the same time intellectually. A return to testing as usual following the pandemic would mean that test-makers, far removed from the teaching and learning context, would continue to yield a detached look at a slice of what a standardized test can reveal.

And frankly, why should stakeholders, as Connell (2013) noted, afford status to a testing practice where "losing has to be legitimated," and "be made credible so not to appear as a matter of unfair discrimination or bad luck?"[3] How to change the status of testing is worthy of more thought and action. Part of change not only requires expanding perspectives, but discovering the more widespread impact of assessment.

What if students and community members had open forums to question the testing tools that so often shape their futures? Often standardized tests are kept hidden from public view riding the excuse that student access to former testing banks might alter the controls of future testing results. And by the time, the results are shared, it is "too late to use them pedagogically."[4] The voices of the test-takers rarely register any complaints, nor are there consistent and valued venues for gathering such qualitative data.

The acceptance of the test-maker's meal tends to be the norm. The test experiences of stakeholders are rarely documented or sought out; certainly, any unsolicited feedback, muted. Where are the five-star ratings for the commercial ACT, SAT, LSAT, or GMAT assessments? It makes sense that if such test results are truly rigorous, then they should also be open to rigorous review. Like everything we do in school, testing practices need to improve, as well; ignoring the source of assessment flaws, by turning up a radio, is not the most astute path to problem solving.

Teachers may have grievance systems in place to voice concerns about all sorts of unhealthy work conditions, but rarely are there proactive measures in place to gain feedback via annual satisfaction and idea-seeking surveys to address what is happening to all students who take part in standardized tests. It is important to ensure that stakeholders have reputable spaces to provide ongoing feedback. Lack of trust can result without a systematic way for gathering and analyzing teacher, family and student experiences within the various school systems.

While school employees are aware of what happens in schools, it is not apparent to parents and other stakeholders what assessment choices can limit learning. School systems can unknowingly take dangerous risks with assessment without making time to understand the potential collateral damage. When schools are careless with student and staff assessment, there are consequences. A transparent culture, however, would mean that the test-makers would be required to communicate with and respond to all voices, or risk further erosion of trust.

Some brave administrators may send out surveys that ask for feedback about curriculum night, parent-teacher conferences, or specific issues that arise, such as parking or child care services. Rarely do leaders collect feedback in systematic ways to determine stakeholder fulfillment of assessment experiences on an annual basis.

How do staff and students really feel about their school? What ideas do students, staff, and families have for improving a school culture, a culture that includes the feedback systems employed? Imagine using a survey to stimulate change and educate employees, clients, parents, and students about other practices? It is rare for questionnaires to include "outlier" ideas, but a survey can play a key role in educating all community members about optional ways of schooling.

Tests and assignments in schools are not independent of curriculum; after all, the content of what is evaluated must come from a body of expectations outlined in classroom, school, and/or authorized government departments of education. What makes an examination of assessment more complicated is the tendency for curriculum designers to load up the expectations, to such a degree that the volume of expectations is unmanageable from a teaching and testing perspective.

Administrators in school systems have yet to ask and respond to tough questions, such as: What understandings are essential? How many subjects should students study at one time? How can all students achieve mastery and be successful? With excessive attention on minutia, it is difficult to see the forest through the trees. With so much to attend to, there is little time to think about how the things we do in schools fit together. It's like making something from IKEA, except all that is provided is the description of the parts, without directions for what to do with them.

The "Romulans" in the *Star Trek* television series used a cloaking device that enabled their vessels to blend in with the infinite number of stars in the universe. Probably unbeknownst to most stakeholders in schools, their "going with the flow" helps to cloak the need to dig deeper to find the source of problems in order to further plan and do something about them. Not everything in school is out of one's control.

Classrooms do not need to be dark and mysterious places. There is much evidence of learning that can and should be gathered in the context of the classroom. Some students can easily demonstrate what they know beyond what a test or assignment can measure. Educators need to include this kind of data as a basis for making evaluative decisions.

Teachers will never be privy to all there is to know; it is possible to gain more insight into student learning, and the relationships between teaching and learning, if cameras were a regular feature in classrooms. The idea of examining videos tends to be met with an "OMG" (Oh My God) response, fearing the eyes of Big Brother peering in on teachers. The distress of looking inside the black box of classrooms has the potential of influencing poor teacher evaluations.

For now, mistrust pretty much grinds the "classcam" as such a data source to a full stop. Even though it might be an incredible way of uncovering student understanding (not captured by pencil and paper tests) or provide clarity for parents about classroom activities, the lack of trust about how such visual data might be used would seem to be a deal-breaker.

In the corporate world, the *Undercover Boss* program showcases people in action, as well as their perspectives, when they are unaware of the masked boss in the room. While it takes incredible courage for these bosses to risk hearing and seeing practices that may undermine the organization and leadership, they do have a unique opportunity to reward foresight, initiative, and hard work. Granted, it would be ideal to have the trust to televise classrooms, but student achievement, for now, relies much more on numerical data, interviews, and other anecdotal information.

It's time to turn the music down, remove the cloaking devices, and listen to what all stakeholders have to say about testing and assessment in schools. Stakeholders do not need to linger in the traditional dog days of assessment; community members can change how schools are viewed. Changing the testing culture is key to making this happen. Paying attention to the volume of tests that young kids face in and outside of school is paramount. The number of tests students endure can be insurmountable. If schools can weed out the excess testing, learning can be more widespread and growth much more sustainable.

Action Items

To learn more about assessment in schools and speak up about the need for change, consider the following testing reform actions:

- *Pause* trusting actions that are not grounded in peer-reviewed research.
- *Pause* assuming that nothing can change.
- *Start* realizing that assessment in schools has flaws.
- *Start* paying attention to news articles about education.
- *Start* asking gritty questions.
- *Study* the impact of the volume, options, and timing of assessment.
- *Study* about conditions that engage students in learning.

What do you think schools need to pause, start, or study?

NOTES

1. Lee, E. (2019), 1.
2. https://www.oecd.org/site/educeri21st/40756908.pdf.
3. Connell, R. (2013), 282.
4. OECD (2013), 160.

2

Truncated Testing

What If?

WHAT IF WE PUMPED THE BRAKES ON STANDARDIZED TESTING?

A standardized test provides truncated data, evidence that represents a sliver of what a student understands. Before engaging in standardized tests, it is important to consider not simply how they function, but their impact in qualitative terms. After all, the aim for gathering educational data should be to improve the quality of schooling.

The OECD (2013) noted that high stakes testing can lead to a distorted view of education that excessively focuses on "distributing repeated practice tests, training students to answer specific types of questions, adopting rote-learning styles of instruction, and allocating more resources to those subjects that are tested." Such an emphasis can lead to schools "focussing more on students near the proficiency cut score and potentially even manipulation of results."[1]

The OECD recommends that "it is important to establish safeguards against excessive emphasis on a particular standardised test and to draw on a range of assessment information to make judgements about learning progress."[2]

Consider the student who reads a math problem that requires several steps to solve. She makes a mistake early on in the calculation, but throughout the remainder of the calculations, the work is accurate. Another student makes mistakes at each stage of the problem. They both fill in an incorrect bubble on the standardized test. They receive the same score. A paper-and-pencil test graded by a classroom teacher would catch what the first student truly knew and, through part marks, the student would be encouraged to continue and perhaps consider a math-related career.

The ease of using a bubble-filling tool may seem efficient, but it is not a comprehensive metric for ranking learners or determining how to teach something better. Schools need to pause and take time to examine such tools and determine how systems can reduce their reliance on such truncated testing.

The unrelenting focus on multiple-choice testing in many North American schools can clearly act as a deterrent to improving teaching and learning. As Berger (2017) claims: "The new national focus on 'standards' seems to be less about high standards than about covering required material, and there is little time left in most schools for the quest for real quality."[3] It's time to recognize standardized tests for what they are—truncated testing—and put the brakes on their over-extended use. It is no longer a convenient truth that it is the ultimate sorter of what's worth knowing and who knows it!

Important decisions should never rely on a single piece of evidence. With so many expectations, it can be difficult for students to have multiple opportunities to demonstrate what they know. A single assignment or test is often the only chance afforded a student. Rarely is there time to gather other evidence of learning, because the overcrowded curriculum makes it close to impossible to re-teach, re-test, or give students every "multi-intelligence" opportunity to showcase their understandings. Community members need to recognize that standardized testing only measures a truncated degree of what students know.

The standardized test tends to be of the multiple-choice kind, which limits the options for demonstrating understandings. Austria, Finland, and Sweden include oral presentations as part of their national assessments.[4] While other forms of assessment can take longer, the results can be much more comprehensive and effective.

University admission directors do not need to elevate the weighing of standardized testing scores for acceptance decisions. The tough decision of selecting students should involve the examination of multiple sources of evidence, rather than the outsourcing of the responsibility to the testing industry. After decades of enduring the additional stressors of SAT and ACT testing, the tide is finally changing; the perception that a university is better if their scores are higher on average than their higher education counterparts is no longer the certain path for admissions.

COVID-19 may have at least temporarily reduced the unwarranted prestige admission teams have placed on standardized test scores. The University of California and its nine undergraduate campuses have chosen to dare greatly and lead the way by removing the SAT and ACT as a factor in student admission selection.

Referring to the temporary suspension during the pandemic of using SAT and ACT scores for admission in hundreds of US colleges and universities, Nietzel (2021) noted that some admission teams "have decided to permanently stop using such tests as part of their admission procedures because of concerns about their possible bias against racial minorities and students from lower-income backgrounds."[5] Based on the size and reputation of this institution, this could be a significant example for other higher education institutions.

Nietzel recognized UC's modelling role: "Its decision to stop using the tests and to give up for now on finding any alternatives to them is expected to lead other institutions to the same conclusion, continuing the anti-test movement that's become a national trend."[6] The pandemic has created an opportunity for universities to move away from requiring standardized tests, but the choice to maintain them as optional does not, as yet, mean their use has been dismissed entirely.

High school teachers, feeling the need to prepare students for college, often try to emulate more teacher-directed learning conditions. Students can often experience more lecture type approaches, typically in the upper grades, minimizing the opportunity for deep learning, interaction, and engagement. When students actually take university courses, they are expected to create original work, figuring out on their own how to independently get there. The need for K-12 educators to make time for critical and creative thinking is imperative in order to build a stronger foundation for success in higher education.

Rather than focus on preparing students for standardized test-taking, a more genuine measure of college readiness should include a body of evidence gathered from interviews, references, high school course work, internships, and a synthesis of experiences within a personal portfolio. Making time to examine qualitative evidence in any form is not an easy task, but who said determining who might be a solid fit had to be easy?

It takes time and hard work for admission teams to make important selection decisions. Research requires triangulated evidence, so how is it that the standardized test, a single piece of evidence with built in gender and racial biases, has been afforded so much status in college admissions for so many years? The hoopla about an ACT and SAT score, seems like misplaced energy, fueling an industry claiming much more than it delivers.

The overemphasis on testing has ambushed the learning culture in many schools. Satirically, this chapter could be titled "Dumb and Dumber" because that's really how so many students feel when they take part in standardized tests. At least half of the students who score below the mid-range feel dumber than the upper half, as they are ranked based on who was fortunate enough to pick the most accurate of the two compelling responses on a multiple-choice test. After memorizing gobs of disconnected standards, half of the participants get to feel inadequate. And they have to pay for it!

To make matters worse many young people in the United States, in particular, have invested hundreds and sometimes thousands of dollars to be bombarded with testing and test preparation materials, all in a hopeful gamble to achieve scores in the top half of the test-taker curve. Lucrative industries have sprung up everywhere to invoice and administer these practice tests and programs. Who truly benefits from the emphasis on this single piece of admission evidence? Follow the money!

There are other standardized tests that are not closely tied to textbook publishers. Tests like the PISA (Program for International Student Assessment) can be considered a more civil measure as it is conducted every four years, with less interruption of teaching and learning. Its claims, however, that the scores indicate potential for economic prosperity have yet to be proven.[7] The PIRLS (Progress in International Reading Literacy Study) and TIMSS (Trends in International Mathematics and Science Study) are also standardized tests that do not make testing the focus on an annual basis.

At what age should young learners be exposed to standardized tests? Only five OECD countries indicated they use central examinations at the primary level: the French Community of Belgium, Canada, Portugal, Turkey, and the United States. Concerned that children, as young as 6 years of age, can elicit failing results in Australia, Tassone (2021) noted: "In countries like Finland and Singapore, which have been identified as high-performing, children do not even begin formal schooling before the age of six or seven."[8]

How can school systems support such accountability measures? In his book, *Testing 3,2,1 What Australians Education Can Learn from Finland*, Lawrence (2020) shares an account of his transformation of thought after examining Finland's education system firsthand. After discussions with Finnish teachers, he admitted that his trust in the Australian NAPLAN (National Assessment Program—Literacy and Numeracy) standardized test and curriculum, was misplaced: "Finnish teachers looked at me as if I were a child molester when I described the NAPLAN tests given to children as young as eight."[9]

Referring to Hargreaves's (2019) message during discussions of the NAPLAN testing at the Gonski Institute forum, Baker (2019) shared that tests such as NAPLAN are "on their last legs around the world, as overseas school systems opt for new assessments that avoid stressing students or stifling learning." Baker added: "Hargreaves said NAPLAN was modelled on tests developed in the 1990s, and countries such as Canada, Israel and Scotland were now acknowledging their unintended impact on students' wellbeing and learning."[10] Standardized testing on its last legs, now that would be progress!

The idea that practice can help improve test scores needs to be revisited by school decision-makers. Imagine how ridiculous it can be for charter schools, for instance, in North America to use test scores to make significant judgments as to which schools to close down or remain open?

Koretz's (2017) book, *The Testing Charade: Pretending to Make Schools Better* revealed his concern for the failures of test-based reform in schools that "fundamentally corrupt the notion of good teaching." He didn't anticipate the level of cheating and scandals that transpired. While he assumed teachers might resort to bad test prep, he didn't foresee that states and districts "would openly peddle it to their teachers." It was unsettling for Koretz to discover "just how much time testing and test prep would swallow or that filling students' time with interim tests and test prep would become the new normal."[11]

The depth and breadth of testing and test prep in many US schools is alarming. Strauss (2019) reported on Darling-Hammond's message about a survey conducted with the Council of the Great City Schools (from 75 US school districts). She indicated that a typical student "took 112 mandated standardized tests between prekindergarten and 12th grade. A testing culture developed in many schools, with excessive test prep and even pep rallies to get kids 'up' for taking their exams."[12] How can such actions be accepted as factors contributing to student achievement?

Notably, while students in the United States "have never scored in the top ranks on PISA or any other international test given since 1964," Tienken (2008) asserted that:

> The United States has outpaced the world in Nobel Prizes in the sciences and medicine since 2000 by a factor of almost 4 (Nobelprize.org, 2013). Ranks on PISA or any other international test do not relate well to economic strength in the G20 countries or overall global competitiveness.[13]

So why do so many US schools continue to place such an emphasis on standardized testing?

Too many students have to endure upwards of three or four practice tests within each school year, missing out on a significant amount of teaching time. Private companies, with their practice test machines, drop in for regular cash grabs, given innocently by trusting school leaders and teachers, believing that their money is well spent. The accountability trolls say things like "We're the good guys," but don't be fooled by the doublespeak. Again, follow the money.

Education can be a public trough that standardized test-makers feast from, often in a truly *Game of Thrones*-type fashion. Testing companies may pay for luncheons and dinners at professional association conferences, but it's time to think carefully about the trade-offs. Student learning, not "testmania," has to come first. An informed public can help take back the lost souls and demand an integrity-based education.

No one can negate the fact that standardized tests interrupt the flow of teaching. Often schools or districts pay for commercial tests so students can have additional practice. These mock testing situations can disrupt upwards of three or four weeks of schooling throughout the year, reducing significantly the teaching time students need. Some charter schools make Fridays their practice test day, serving up obese portions of multiple-choice meals, that tempt food comas of the test fatigue kind, especially when students have to endure so many tests before the one that counts at the year end. Such madness is simply dumb and dumber!

The echoing response to those who challenge standardized tests tends to go something like this: "These tests are objective; even though they are not perfect, they are all we've got." Let's unpack some of these assumptions and truths. First of all, who says these tests are objective? Many multiple-choice options reveal two solid understandings, yet one of the responses is considered most correct. How often do students get to examine the tests and their answers, to learn from their supposed mistakes?

Standardized tests are also kept hidden from parents; they are not permitted to view questions or answers. If it happens at all, it is rare. Everyone, including many teachers, are expected to be compliant by trusting the process and findings.

Rigorous standards have been developed to guide and test the strength of a test. The American Educational Research Association (AERA), the American Psychological Association (APA), and National Council on Measurement in Education (NCME) collaborated to develop *Standards for Educational and Psychological Testing,* a trusted resource in 1999. According to the OECD (2013), "responsible professional practice in educational assessment" can be ensured when test-makers respect a number of principles regarding the appropriate use of assessment results.[14]

The OECD (2013) claimed that assessment should provide "multiple opportunities for students to take alternate forms of an assessment." They added that it is important to consider substituting alternative measures of test scores "especially when tests are likely to give a deceptively low indication of a student's achievement because of test anxiety or disabilities that may reduce the validity of standardised test results." They added that students must have "had opportunities to learn the material that they are being assessed on (AERA, APA and NCME, 1999; Baker and Linn, 2004 . . .)."[15]

What does it look like when mistakes lead to learning? Leah Alcala, a seventh-grade math teacher at King Middle School in Berkeley, California, does not put a grade on tests or assignments immediately. Rather, the class focuses on "favorite mistakes" when their work is returned. It is not until after a dive into what can be confusing, do students actually receive their scores.[16]

When you examine some test questions and answers, it can be argued more often than not that two answers were strong choices for identifying the central idea in a paragraph, or the conflict in a piece of fictional poetry. When there are two close answers, it is clearly a subjective choice of the test-maker. Think of the millions of standardized tests taken, and the number of students who might pick the other correct answer—and how their lives are affected by the test results.

If test designers were so confident about these tools, the questions would not exist behind an iron curtain, banning the option of reviewing answers. Students need to learn from mistakes, so holding firm to the excuse that they need to keep banks of questions secret, seems to be a lame retort.

The raw data from standardized tests are often difficult for laypeople to follow. By designing complicated layers of analysis, it is possible to make the statistics dance in a number of directions. Findings can be oversimplified in executive summaries that rarely espouse the degree of reliability of the scores. Furthermore, it is questionable how assessors of essays and short answers on some standardized tests can be trusted to come up with comparative results.

Even when standardized tests include short answers and essays, with elaborate moderation systems of repeated viewings and pre-scoring checks, the range of responses can be inconsistent.

Claims that parents can be assured that student work is assessed via a standard is one thing, but trusting 1,200 markers, as in the case of the EQAO (Education Quality and Accountability Office)[17] to interpret the link between the student work and the standards the same way is a huge stretch. It is not uncommon for 50% of the raters of a piece of writing to score it as a 2 out of 4, while close to 50% of the reviewers would give the same piece of writing a 3 rating. How sound is it to average these two ratings? Furthermore, stakeholders need to ask the tough question: How accountable is the assessment itself?

The OECD (2013) recognizes the intent of moderation as "a set of approaches that aim to ensure the quality and comparability of assessment judgement." This process relies on a systematic approach to assessing data whereby teachers may engage in "cross-marking each other's assessments or discussing student performance in groups," or student work may be assessed by "a competent external organisation systematically checking school-based marking." The objective of moderation is to "reduce variations in the ways teachers assess students and set marks in order to achieve fairness in student assessment and reporting."[18]

It is important to develop guidelines that "emphasise the importance of moderation as a process for developing assessment confidence and common understandings of assessment standards among teachers, but also as a mechanism to increase the dependability (validity and reliability) of teacher assessments of student performance." The process can be an engaging professional growth activity for teachers when they discuss student work samples. Social moderation can happen when colleagues and students examine assessment criteria.[19]

The Linkage Project used psychometric scaling and online moderation to target teacher assessment capability "using scaled annotated exemplars of achievement standards in online moderation." The project included the development of "scaled work samples exemplifying A-E standards of achievement . . . and a new approach to moderating teacher judgements."[20] It would be interesting to consider the possibility of using fewer standards, such as A, B, and Not Yet to see if this might improve moderation efforts and enhanced teacher capacity for assessing students.

What would happen if markers were given three, rather than five, letter choices (Linkage Project) or the four choices in the case of the EQAO writing assessment? If there was 90% agreement among markers that a piece of writing does "not meet," "meets" or "exceeds expectations," then the tool with fewer qualifiers would appear more objective.

Subjectivity increases, with more options for evaluating the quality of work. Furthermore, many educators assume that 100 qualifier options in the form of percentages is more objective, but the more room teachers have to determine a score, the more such assessments lack a consistent application and increase the level of subjectivity.

A standardized test worthy of use needs to account for a number of internal statistical checks including: test-retest reliability, confirmatory factor analysis, and convergent reliability, to name a few. If such tests are not transparent and subject to their own tests of rigor, their importance needs to be revisited.

The OECD (2013) defines transparency as "the degree to which information is available regarding expected learning outcomes, the criteria that will be used in judging student learning and the rules being applied when judgements are made about learning."[21] It also matters how the test results are used. Usability, as defined by the OECD "refers to how policy makers, school leaders, teachers, parents and students make sense of and respond to assessment results."[22]

The design of student assessment should be timely, easy to understand and interpret for teachers and/or students, and instructionally useful "to guide subsequent, intended decision making and action."[23] An additional concern of standardized tests is they have time limits. Not only do students need to read the mind of the test-maker, they have to be a speedy "greyhound" test-taker. Many standardized tests do not provide enough time to determine what students know. The results illustrate more how fast students know responses, not if they know all the responses. Some students need more time than standardized tests permit.

Students identified with special needs can often apply through a deliberately onerous process to receive more time to write standardized tests. How is it that only students with special needs can access more time? All students who have the capacity to answer the questions should be given the time they need to do so. Yet, the test-makers deem that the conditions must be the same. All students must complete the test in a designated time, even if it means the results of the tests do not accurately portray what young people know. We can't taint the process, but we can taint the results . . . Really?

Standardized tests have wagged the tail of the dog for far too long. If time is such a precious commodity, let's use it to help make better decisions regarding assessment, college admission, and various kinds of mastery certification. Let's increase the status of 11th and 12th grades, especially because they represent teacher accounts on student report cards.

University presidents, admission teams, future employers, and school accreditors/auditors can demand the use of more formal interviews and examinations of portfolios to learn more about student passions and assets, as well as their extracurricular and volunteer involvement. Serious attention can be paid to references. Young people can be taught early on that their reputation and experiences matter, something the workforce values.

If you ask people what made a difference in their lives, there is a good chance they would speak of a teacher who believed in them. No one would probably say their path to success was the Euclid Mathematics Contest,[24] or the SAT. Perhaps there needs to be more qualitative research unpacking what Nobel Peace Prize recipients or Rhodes Scholars think mattered to them? We need to rethink the weighting and value of standardized tests.

The research on asset and strength building, as well as a host of predictive index reporting tools that narrow specific dispositions for particular lines of work or study, can be much more informative than conventional standardized tests. Currently, most college admissions officers are not required to have a background in education or assessment, so it may seem easier to simply trust standardized test scores as the most reliable metric for differentiating applicants.

It is more time-consuming to meet with potential applicants to review a full assortment of qualitative and quantitative data, but such a process would have more integrity than narrow test scores. Universities miss out on potential talent when they screen applicants for a baseline SAT or ACT standardized test score. Testing worshippers actually believe standardized test scores represent one's capacity for school success, teacher talent, and student achievement. Many colleges and universities advertise their average entrance SAT and ACT scores, as badges of honor, yet few people recognize their inherent flaws.

It is a stretch to assume there is alignment between test scores, intelligence, and creative and critical thinking. How is the College Board,[25] which owns the SAT, linked in any way to legitimate research-based academia? And why does it matter that the US News agency has such status in ranking colleges and universities based on critical masses of SAT scores? How the data can dance when people do not pay close attention to the examiners and distributors of "best national university rankings."

There will be many devoted consumers who will swear that the merits of standardized tests include problem-solving, and therefore contribute to critical and creative thinking. However, the problems that live and breathe inside such tests have already well-defined solutions. Do people breathe a sigh of relief knowing the future of our planet will be in the hands of graduates who have been tested to know and regurgitate what is already known, quickly? Contrary, to the faith placed in such intelligence strainers, graduates should be expected to do more than perform well on time-limited tests.

There is inherent gender and racial bias in standardized tests. The OECD (2013) recommended offering different assessment formats and tasks (e.g., test-based, performance-tasks, oral, written)."[26] Dadani (2019) claimed that high stakes testing "contradicts the new shift in education which speaks of differentiated learning styles, multiple intelligences, and providing options on assignments that test student understanding, skills, and knowledge of curriculum learned." He added that standardized tests can be biased in how they are framed, delivered, and scored and can "even prevent a student from living the good life."[27]

In Canada, the Ontario government commissioned the Ontario Institute for Studies in Education's (OISE) Carol Campbell and a team of experts to make recommendations about the EQAO. Rather than support large-scale testing, their report indicated that some form of testing should provide an overview or snapshot for purposes of informing and guiding educators and government officials. They also recommended the elimination of the grade 3 test, and replacing the grade 9 math test and grade 10 literacy test with a grade 10 assessment combining literacy, numeracy, and other skills.[28]

The culture of many charter schools in the United States revolves around the test. How they would be ranked and if their doors would remain open—all hanging on test scores, and to a lesser extent attendance and re-enrollment data. Even though it is logical that sustainable change should take three to five years to stick, all roads still lead to that short-term test in May. The tsunami of practice tests culminating in the single end-of-year "do or die" experience perpetuates a hopeless and anxious culture among staff, students, and parents.

There may be a few indoctrinated educators who believe standardized testing is an invigorating and rigorous experience, but nothing could be further from the truth. A world focused on the past cannot find solutions to tomorrow's problems. The answers to climate change, cures for cancer, or methods of space travel to different galaxies, do not exist today. The only dedicated space on a multiple-choice test is for what is already known. Yet, there are so many other tools and classroom experiences that can generate evidence of creativity and critical thinking.

Schools can do better than putting their eggs in a total recall high stakes testing culture. Ask teachers what life was like in their schools leading up to "the" test. Ask them about the lifeless morale in the post-test month of June.

What happened to the last month of school when the days were filled with fun review, teacher-student softball games, barbecues, and a full force of energy dedicated to planning for the next school year? By the time June rolls around, teachers and students are so spent they have little interest left for fun, review, or future planning.

To new teachers in the field, this may sound like a memory from a visit to Oz, not the schools they endure during and after the annual testing burden. High stakes testing simply sucks the fun out of the culture. At the turn of the century in the United States, there seemed to be a jarring lack of trust in teachers, coupled with a blind faith in standardized testing. Accountability trends flooded schools in the United States, followed by Canada and the United Kingdom.

The increased need for behavior management also hinges on and is escalating by the pressures to perform well on such tests. If school boards or state/provincial level leaders do not trust teachers and require standardized benchmark data for auditing purposes, then why not check it at the beginning of the year, so teachers can use the benchmark data as diagnostic evidence to guide their planning? And why, for dog's sake, do these tests have to be issued every year?

The timing of tests, whether delivered during standardized test weeks or even at the classroom level, is an arbitrary point in time that identifies one sliver of learning evidence. It would be timely to have further discussions about the timing of standardized and classroom tests, especially in a digital age when we could have more options, like micro-credentialing and running records of mastery achievement. What research grounds the timing and volume of standardized tests?

Weston (2018) noted concerns that "EQAO testing does not achieve its goals and, in fact, hinders learning outcomes, especially in marginalized student populations."[29] Like other high stakes tests, the province of Ontario requires all students to sit the test, regardless of whether they have been identified with special needs, or are newcomers to the English language, or not.

There is no equal distribution of students in schools that require special needs or ELL (English Language Learning) support, so this disequilibrium alone makes such findings tenuous. Furthermore, there are many students that remain on referral lists for psych-ed assessments, often for several years. Apart from the need to account for differentiated language and intellectual needs, there are many students in varying proportions at different schools who are disadvantaged by social-emotional and physical limitations.

The results of standardized tests clearly confirm the research that links low socioeconomic factors to decreases in vocabulary and reading comprehension.[30] Weston (2018) noted: "Schools in wealthier areas tend to have higher EQAO scores than schools in lower socioeconomic areas. This is why real estate agents use EQAO test scores to sell residential property—to assess the socioeconomic status of a neighbourhood."[31]

One could argue that there were times when there were considerable variances in how well schools addressed state or provincial expectations, so the need for some type of litmus test did arouse some interest from the community and educators inside schools. Weston and many others, who defy the current norm of testing, have revealed many serious flaws in high stakes tests.

Many members of the public are convinced that such scores are solid measures of student understanding. With such public support, the tide has shifted from a lack of accountability supposedly in the seventies to "this is the way we always do it" today. There it is again, that undertone of "we can't change it anyway." Argh!

Stepping back and reviewing educational research can reveal patterns of meaningful studies in the seventies that spawned a number of best practice findings; many such initiatives, unfortunately, lost key momentum when the culture of high stakes testing was ushered in. Educators should not lose sight of ideal teaching and learning practices.

The recommendations in a typical psycho-educational report often reintroduce educators to solid methods of teaching left behind. Psychologists see the benefits and promise of such practices (talk, choice, self-assessment, co-investigations, board games, peer teaching, internships, volunteerism, camp) and, therefore, recommend them to help kids who feel marginalized in classrooms fit in.

Often the word "innovation" is reserved for those who can design software for multiple-choice tests, but it is the psychologists—and their desire to help one identified student at a time—who are leading the charge to support more effective instructional choices. They are well aware that a one-size-fits-all model does not work for the ever-growing critical mass of students identified with special needs. They also know that the sameness model seems to only be valued by the students showing upper quadrant success.

Ever since the testing culture has taken hold, school principals want to know what to do to accommodate and support students and teachers in special education. Could it be that the lack of growth of truly innovative curriculum and instruction has contributed to the increasing number of kids who opt out in class or have special needs? This is one of those tough questions. Many readers most likely have kids in the upper quadrants, so unpacking such a big picture may not, at first glance, seem to matter, but it does.

Nevertheless, it can be a struggle for parents to keep their kids in the upper quadrant. The sharp rise in demand for spaces in private or independent schools, the popular practice of in-home tutors at the dining room table, and the commonplace interaction with Khan Academy[32] and other YouTube instructors is testimony to the fact that the six hours a day of schooling is not working as well as it should.

The testing machine costs taxpayers billions and billions of dollars to construct and implement, money that could have been dedicated to reducing class sizes and giving teachers more time to help students consolidate understandings. In Ontario alone, the costs of EQAO testing is over $30,000,000; children testing three times in their education career come close to spending $100,000,000 in their school lifetime.[33] Now think about the numbers of students and the pattern of annual testing in the United States, and how exponentially these costs rise.

In an article titled "Testing Is Not the Way Forward" in *CommonWealth Magazine*, Shirley (2021) noted that advocates for standardized testing "have been on the defensive because the tests failed to improve student achievement as promised by reformers." He added that "the rise of the testing industry was correlated with growing rates of anxiety and depression among young people," and that "testers aggravated rather than ameliorated differences in achievement among racial and ethnic groups, and between social classes,"[34] adding unlimited costs associated with health and well-being.

Testing, together with the massive volume of expectations, has not only interrupted the widespread use of effective instructional practices, it has left many students on the curb, lost, anxious, and, in many cases, angry. As a public increasingly becomes more and more interested in education, stakeholders should expect more than the retort "That's the way we always do it." A democratic society can do more than sit, lie down, roll over, or shake a paw.

Stakeholders can examine what propels and incentivizes the standardized test world. Schools can review the money spent on cycles of testing in terms of the design, implementation, analysis, and follow-through. More stakeholders can weigh in on what could be a waste of time, resources, and money.

Schools must also be cautious about the pandemic fixes. As Selwyn (2021) claims: "Critical education scholars . . . need to be hypervigilant of the ways in which COVID-19 will be misused to force radical education reforms by those who stand to profit directly from them."[35] The promises of efficiency and often free services in advance of more sustained financial commitments enables non-experts in education to use technology as a way in to shifting the goals and control of schooling.

The testing and data dashboard culture in some schools may provide some temporary ease of management; however, the profitable gains ensued by such encroachment that can take hold over school systems needs to be further examined. Hogan and Williamson (2021) raised concerns about the private sector, specifically global technology companies bringing commercial agendas to public education. They noted: "The provision of digital infrastructure for on-line teaching and learning . . . data storage, management, and analytics (e.g., Microsoft 365, Google G Suite, and Amazon Cloud)"[36] can make a school vulnerable to outside controls.

COVID-19 has created a perfect storm, keeping school leaders fixated on developing and implementing safety protocols and policies. With so much to address, it is easier for businesses to profit from such vulnerability. In Sellar's (2021) provocation, he suggested: "The pandemic has certainly created new opportunities for commercial actors to benefit from the disruption of schooling and higher education."[37]

As a principal, the freeness and access to Zoom immediately upon government-mandated school closure was indeed embraced. However, as Wan (2020) noted, educators need to be aware of the "support now, sell later"[38] potential that lock schools into subscriptions plans.

There is much to learn about classroom assessment and the unreliable often grandiose glossy packages brought on by the testing companies and recommendations by non-educators with way too much control over inner-city school education. Gathering benchmark data can be very helpful, especially if using a dependable standardized tool. All tests have limitations but there are tests that can yield recommendations that can support individual needs of students.

The results of the Woodcock-Johnson III[39] and the Weschler[40] tests, for instance, focus on what the students know—and if there are any disabilities that require different methods for learning. Good special education teachers should be qualified to administer such tests on an individual basis. Such comprehensive tests are typically not completed in one sitting but are spread out over several days.

The Woodcock-Johnson III Test of Achievement assesses measures of reading/oral fluency as well as mathematics, written language skills, and general knowledge. The Weschler Individual Achievement Test III measures reading, math, and written language and oral language skills.

Is it possible for all students to take part in psycho-educational testing at reasonable intervals throughout their school experience? Could such tests inform teaching practices and curriculum design? While not intended to function in such ways, such data could provide some compelling comparative metrics that may support, or not, the results and need for so many overused standardized tests.

So, what can be done differently than the current pattern of testing insanity? First of all, there is no need to take an annual state, national, or provincial test, especially written by publishers. The curriculum must not be focused on test preparation. Good teachers can identify if the students have at least three pieces of evidence that proves mastery. This can be a test, a project, or a presentation. A quality program includes differentiation and differentiated needs to be reflected in the instructional and assessment choices.

If schools gather benchmark/diagnostic data through tools such as the Woodcock-Johnson or the Weschler, when students arrive they can rely on the teacher/administrator (who monitors the teachers) to gather the interim data of mastery, and then redo the same diagnostic test three years later—to see the transformation and change based on small class sizes, tutoring, and quality curriculum. Why would there be a need for testing at the end of each school year?

Having a curriculum and talented teachers who can transform learning (over time) could be a key to providing a solid education. Testing does not need to happen every year. What is done year after year to students in so many schools in the United States does not make sense. Tests pulled together for mass distribution, typically by writers for the publishing industry, is like using Morse code to teach how to communicate on the web. Too much is a stake. It may be enough that students can take an international test to see how the curriculum and the students fair globally.

The politicizing of high stakes tests and the linking of their results to annual funding makes it impossible for schools and teachers to create conditions for ideal teaching and learning. Too many students are fed the same practice testing in between the annual testing with the assumption that the results will change. This popular menu in charter schools has probably increased the number of students graduating from high school, but it is not preparing them for the world of college and work.

When the curriculum is set by testing standards, then thinking is compromised—the exact skill necessary to succeed in university and in future careers. Good enough will not lead to real change. When decision-makers take a shortcut around the research into classroom assessment, it is difficult to change the learning landscape. It's time to pump the brakes and slow down the rapid testing, so educators can reduce the content load and accelerated impact of skimming the surface of learning.

To have time for deep learning, educators need to re-purpose how instructional time is afforded to learning, rather than testing and memorizing random facts. So how can community members, inside and outside the walls of our schools, help to turn down the volume on high stakes testing to make room for more meaningful accountability measures and honor more effective instructional practices?

Action Items

Ask decision-makers and the public, who pay their salaries, if they can pause, start, or study to engage the following:

- *Pause* testing in every grade. Think about beginning the testing at the start of the middle school grades and then again at the beginning of high school.
- *Pause* practice testing and purchasing of practice test booklets.
- *Pause* averaging in scores from students new to the English language.
- *Pause* averaging in scores from students identified with special needs.
- *Pause* ranking teachers and schools based on testing results.
- *Start* building multi-intelligence expectations within your rubrics and testing tools.
- *Start* testing at the beginning of a school year so data can be used for diagnostic purposes to inform curriculum planning and instruction.
- *Start* developing questions that are not intended to trick students.
- Start reading about the limitations of standardized testing (i.e., https://www.fairtest.org/whats-wrong-standardized-tests; https://rethinkingschools.org/articles/the-gathering-resistance-to-standardized-tests/)
- *Study* perceptions of test-takers and teachers and do something about the recommendations.
- *Study* the lessons from Finland—(i.e., Meet Pasi Sahlberg's *Reimagine Schools* podcast) https://podcasts.apple.com/gb/podcast/finnish-lessons-with-dr-pasi-sahlberg/id1397680693?ii=1000492848675).

What would you like decision-makers to pause, start, or study? What do you think might happen if schools reduced the importance of standardized testing?

NOTES

1. OECD (2013), 217.
2. Ibid.
3. Berger, R. (2017), https://my.pblworks.org/resource/document/beautiful_work.
4. Ibid., 179.
5. Nietzel, M.T. (2021), https://www.forbes.com/sites/michaeltnietzel/2021/12/13/the-top-ten-higher-education-stories-of-2021/?sh=78fffa373561.
6. Ibid.
7. Tienken, C.H. (2013), 156.
8. Tassone, M. (November 21, 2021), https://theconversation.com/a-failure-at-6-data-driven-assessment-isnt-helping-young-childrens-learning-169463.

9. Lawrence, M. (2020), 8.
10. Baker, J. (March 10, 2019), 1, https://www.smh.com.au/education/on-its-last-legs-why-the-world-is-abandoning-naplan-style-tests-20190308-p512v4.html.
11. Koretz, D. (2017), 243.
12. Strauss, V. (March 4, 2019), https://www.washingtonpost.com/education/2019/03/04/if-all-that-testing-had-been-improving-us-we-would-have-been-highest-achieving-nation-world-heres-what-does-work-school-reform/.
13. Tienken, C. H. (2008), 14.
14. Ibid., 209–210.
15. Ibid.
16. Schwartz, K. (November 15, 2018), https://www.kqed.org/mindshift/52456/a-grading-strategy-that-puts-the-focus-on-learning-from-mistakes.
17. http://osslt.eqao.com/scores.html.
18. Ibid.,185.
19. Ibid.
20. Adie, L., Wyatt-Smith, C., & Haynes, M. (2020).
21. Ibid., 142.
22. Ibid.
23. Ibid.
24. https://www.cemc.uwaterloo.ca/contests/euclid.html.
25. www.US News.com.
26. Ibid., 222.
27. Dadani, S. (2019), 165–166. https://tspace.library.utoronto.ca/bitstream/1807/97346/1/Dadani_Sharmin_201911_EdD_thesis.pdf.
28. Campbell, C., Clinton, J., Fullan, M., Hargreaves, A., James, C., & Longboat, K.D. (March 2018).
29. Weston, D. (November 16, 2018), https://heartandart.ca/?p=7004.
30. Perkins, S. C., Finegood, E. D., & Swain, J. E. (2013), 10. https://www.ncbi.nlm.nih.gov/pmc/articles/PMC3659033/.
31. Ibid.
32. https://www.khanacademy.org.
33. Ibid.
34. Shirley, D. (July 5, 2021), https://commonwealthmagazine.org/opinion/standardized-testing-is-not-the-way-forward/.
35. Selwyn, N. (2021). p. 203.
36. Hogan, A., & Williamson, B. (2021), 210.
37. Sellar, S. (2021), 214.
38. Wan, T. (2020), https://www.edsurge.com/news/2020-04-07-traffic-is-booming-for-online-education-providers-but-so-are-costs.
39. https://riversideinsights.com/woodcock_johnson_iv.
40. https://www.child-psychologist.com.au/wechsler-intelligence-scale-for-children.html.

3

Reporting Reform

What If?

WHAT IF REPORTING PRACTICES DO NOT EVOLVE?

How educators document learning for students, parents, and the system matters. Just as a progressive school or school system is committed to improving teaching practices, so should we accept new ways to improve reporting practices. Many educators can be reluctant to change because it seems good enough to keep what people are used to in place. Many experts might challenge such claims that hinge on the assumption that if it's not broken, don't fiddle with it. Reporting practices, like every other learning support, should evolve; if they remain the same, they cannot improve.

The general system of awarding A through F grades has been a fixture for over a century in many North American elementary schools. High schools and post-secondary institutions tend to use specific percentages, ranging from 0 to 100. Most educators recognize that a norm-referenced approach to reporting focuses on ranking students, whereas a criterion-referenced system acknowledges all students who meet specific learning criteria.

It is common practice in colleges and universities to "bell up" or "bell down" the results of tests so the average looms near 68%. If the average was 85% in a course, evidence indicating that the average student knew that much, these students would receive a "belled" score of 68%. Inversely, if the average grade was 45%, the average student would be belled up to 68%. In both cases the results do not accurately reflect what the students know.

Why do the grades need to change if a critical mass of students achieved high grades? They should be proud of their accomplishments, and the teachers who prepared them should also be celebrated. If the average score in a course was 45%, then the students need better teaching and learning opportunities;

after all the students paid tuition to learn, and such a score does not reflect substantive learning or teaching.

Ideally students should be evaluated based on their own merit, not relative to the performance of their peers. Kohn (2019) noted that "success seems to matter only if it is attained by a few." By evaluating people "relative to each other . . . even if everyone has done quite well, or improved over time, half will always fall below the median—and look like failures." He added "the point isn't to do well but to defeat other people who are also trying to do well."[1]

Kohn (2019) claimed: "A school's ultimate mission, apparently, is not to help everyone learn but to rig the game so there will always be losers."[2] Returning to such normalcy of accountability, post COVID-19, would be a serious mistake.

Recognizing that traditional grading systems are usually not consistent, O'Connor (2017) challenges educators to rethink dated grading practices. He noted that the lack of assessment guidance for teachers can lead to a "highly individual, idiosyncratic practice whereby two students achieving at the same level might receive very different grades."[3] He claimed that "a single grade for a subject does nothing more than provide a general impression of the student's performance." Schools can do better.

Standards-based grading (SBG) is a more recent option being implemented in some elementary and secondary schools. Rather than a single grade for each subject, specific standards within each subject are addressed within such standards-aligned reporting tools. O'Connor noted: "Teachers who implement standards-based grading and reporting consistently say it contributes to a learning culture . . . students become self-directed learners who have a much more positive attitude about school and learning."[4] These report cards address items that tend to focus on governmental-defined expectations.

Technically, a standards-based report card should include all standards that students are taught in a particular course; however, it makes sense to determine which expectations are more essential, so that teachers can focus attention on deeper understandings of fewer items. Less is more!

The problem for most jurisdictions is that there are too many standards listed for each subject each year. Such a report card featuring the Common Core State Standards, for instance in grade 4 English, might need to list upwards of 70-plus expectations. Imagine a parent or student reviewing pages and pages of results? On the one hand, the traditional report card that scrunches together every part of math into a single average score would not suffice as specific quality feedback; on the other hand, evaluating all expectations can seem unwieldly.

The idea of identifying fewer essential standards for each subject in each grade can help provide a more robust feedback mechanism, as well as afford clearer directions for improvement. One US charter school featured a sample of an "essential" standards-based report card for mathematics (Table 3.1) that also included differentiated options.

Determining fewer essential, yet rigorous, expectations is key to making such standards-based reporting manageable. Including the related expectations for previous or next grades enables readers to realize how expectations link to one another.

The grade 2 Science portion of the report card was shorter as there were fewer hours allotted for instruction. The Science report included the following expectations: Asks questions to reveal a sense of wonder; Records interesting questions about science experiments in science log; Draws diagrams showing details of scientific findings; Uses scientific language to share ideas about what might cause things to happen; and Demonstrates an understanding of how parts can make a whole.

The English Language Arts (ELA) part of the overall report was also another page in length. Other subjects that did not require the same kind of progressive content and skills did not require as many items in order to achieve subject-related mastery. Such report cards can be quite comprehensive with each subject represented, and can run up to four and five pages in length.

In a comprehensive collection of research on grading practices called "A Century of Grading Research: Meaning and Value in the Most Common Educational Measure," Brookhart et al. (2016) noted the following limitation: "Teachers implementing SBG reported that it took longer to record the detailed information included in the SBG report cards but felt the additional time was worthwhile because SBGs yielded higher-quality information."[5]

Tracking and assessing individual skills can take more time, and such a report card is lengthier, but the communication of what has been learned can be much more precise. O'Connor (2017) claimed that teachers who use standards-based grading and reporting "consistently say it contributes to a learning culture, in place of the traditional grading/point accumulation culture, and that students become self-directed learners who have a much more positive attitude about school and learning."[6]

Notably absent on these sample differentiated report cards (Table 3.1) is the use of percentages, which are more frequently used to rank students. The use of percentages on report cards gives the illusion of precision and provides an opportunity to present distinguished numbers showcasing the "top dogs," but the use of an A or an A+ to evaluate student work or a grade is much more accurate—as a grade grouping of percentages has a higher likelihood of being replicated by another teacher.

In addition to removing percentages, a sound report card should not include class or course medians, as they serve no purpose in supporting or enhancing

Table 3.1: Grade 2 Essential Standards-Based (and Differentiated) Math Report Card

Differentiated Math Report Card—Grade 2   Name: _____
Foundational Skill/Understanding (Grade 1)
Grade Skill/Understanding Focus (Grade 2)
Enriched Skill/Understanding (Grade 3)

Areas	NY = Not Yet
Place Value	Order numbers & use place value between 0-100
	Order numbers & use place value between 0–1000
	Order numbers & use place value within 0 to 1 million
Number Forms	Identify & differentiate between odd & even numbers
	Compare numbers to 1000 using >, <, or =
	Use expanded form from written to whole numbers
Operations	Add & subtract within 100
	Add & subtract at least four digit numbers
	Multiply & divide within one digit numbers (distributive property)
Number Patterns	Skip count by 2, 5, & 10
	Make patterns with repeated addition, 1-5
	Identify multiples of 1 through 5
Part Numbers	Divide shapes into equal quarters using images & objects
	Divide shapes into thirds & sixths in relation to the whole
	Use number lines to add, subtract, & find equivalent fractions with like denominators
3D Geometry	Describe the difference between squares & rectangles
	Identify, describe, & classify 3D figures
	Identify objects using edges, sides, & corners of 3D objects
Measurement in Geometry	Trace & identify sides of 2D shapes and sides and faces of 3D objects
	Find perimeter of polygons
	Find area using length & width & compare area to perimeter
Measurement in Science	Measure lines of symmetry in 2D figures using centimeters (cm)
	Compare millimeters (mm) & meters (m) to centimeters (cm) using <, >, & =
	Round, estimate, & apply units from metric & US customary, both whole & part measures
Data Management in Research/Inquiry	Organize, represent, & interpret data up to 3 or 4 categories
	Draw & analyze pictograph & bar graph with up to 4 categories
	Construct, compare, & synthesize frequency tables & fractal line plots (focus on median)

future learning. At least half of the families reviewing such a report can feel a sense of relief that their child is not in the bottom half of the class, but how can knowing that a score is in the lower portion of a class help motivate anyone to do better? The purpose of such a metric may be the conversation for a cocktail party, but it serves little to no purpose as value-added data.

Fewer qualifiers increase objectivity; whereas report cards with more qualifier options increase the range of options, making the grades less consistent and more subjective. Fairness matters to students, so using tools that make sense to them should be a consideration. Standards-based reports can be an alternative with a reduced number of qualifiers. A differentiated standards-based report card does not include traditional Cs or Ds or a 1–2–3–4 rating scheme.

The differentiated standard-based math report card (Table 3.1) measures the quality of the degree of mastery, revealing a more consistent level of excellence for A work, proficient levels of achievement for a B score, with A+ being warranted for exceptional and exemplary work. Students did not have an opportunity to "leave learning behind" with an achievement of a C, D, or F grade.

The "Not Yet" indicators did not disappear into an abyss of tasks, not completed. The tasks remained on the students' customized reports until they were able to demonstrate mastery of at least a B or proficient level. Rather than the focus on the "top dog," the reporting focus can shift to all students. "Top dogs" can work ahead on next grade challenges, while students who require more support still can work at foundational skills until they are ready to master the grade level expectations.

Many standard-based report cards tend to use four qualifiers; most common are *advanced, proficient, basic,* and *below basic.* Determining whether work is basic or proficient is often difficult for different educators to replicate results. Likewise, achievement on report cards that feature 1–2–3–4 can run into similar consistency issues. Such grading is intended to present a uniform process for teacher grading. Even when hours and hours of professional development time has been dedicated to helping teachers distinguish between work that is evaluated as below, approaching, and meeting standards, it is still difficult for different teachers to replicate the same scores.

In the world of work, there are companies that use a four-tier appraisal system to rank their employees in one of four quadrants. Employees in the top quartile would be awarded bonuses and be tagged for future promotions. Employees in the bottom quartile would not be considered as upwardly mobile and are often vulnerable to lay-offs. Like such companies, schools and admission teams who look at students through such a ranking lens miss an opportunity to increase the critical mass of high performers.

At one time report cards used to include effort scores for each grade, but nowadays these scores are generalized as part of a list of learning skills. Such skills may be addressed in simple checklist form or include separate qualifiers such as "needs improvement," "satisfactory," "good," or "excellent." Such grades are often determined at the time the report card is being filled out by the teacher. Administrators rarely expect teachers to track evidence of learning skills in a grade book.

Unlike other subjects that require at least three pieces of evidence throughout the term, social and emotional learning expectations seem to be treated as less important "soft skills," not requiring a grade like other subjects deemed more important. As a result, some parents may view learning skills as sub-par, unless they are looking to see if a behavior pattern has influenced a poor grade in a particular subject area.

Notwithstanding, social and emotional skills do play an important role in the world of work and life. Simply from an equity standpoint, why would schools change the assessment metrics when providing feedback about any form of learning? The idea that learning skills are measured differently than other conventional subjects is worthy of further discussion.

According to Brookhart et al. (2016), accounts of student behavior are referred to as "non-achievement factors." They note that "teachers idiosyncratically use a multitude of achievement and non-achievement factors in their grading practices to improve learning and motivation as well as document academic performance." Their research found that effort is a key part of grading that teachers use to help students achieve high grades, and in doing so, teacher judgment is considered "an essential part of fair and accurate grading."[7]

The mixing of achievement and how the students come to understand is referred to as a multidimensional measure. Significant research supports the idea that multidimensional grading links more to future success than testing scores (Rumberger, 1987; Cairns, Cairns, & Neckerman, 1989; Hargis, 1990; Nichols & Berliner, 2007; Cliffordson, 2008; Atkinson & Geiser, 2009; Polikoff, Porter, & Smithson, 2011).

Those who negate the value of teacher grades in the context of their own classrooms need to think about the merit of including such insight. As noted by Brookhart et al. (2016): "Many teachers use their understanding of individual student circumstances, their instructional experience, and perceptions of equity, consistency, accuracy, and fairness to make professional judgments, instead of solely relying on a grading algorithm."[8]

Recognizing that "grading practices may vary within a single classroom," and between teachers, they are confident that teacher input is not a problem, but valued "as a needed element of accurate, fair grading."[9] College and university admission teams face a real challenge when it comes to selecting candidates for programs. What strategies are being employed to enhance objectivity beyond reliance on entrance or SAT/ACT testing?

Furthermore, admission teams should be aware that even though teacher bias can be a grading limitation, so too can researcher bias and test designer bias, which can influence the construction of test questions and interpretation of test results. Making time to review report cards and interview candidates while considering their portfolios and experiences should help enhance admission decisions and be more comprehensive than comparing numerical scores.

Strong teachers recognize the links between knowing science and acting like a scientist. Their grading can embed behaviors of experts such as historians, mathematicians, and engineers. Given the important role teacher's play in the context of learning, their judgment should matter.

Macdonald (2004) claimed that assessment should emulate professional contexts that students may find themselves in the future, "showing how they cope with acting and thinking like a nurse, physicist or historian and the lifelong learning skills needed to continue to develop in these changing professional areas."[10]

Recognizing that report cards are limited, Spear (2019) noted that the students' results do not necessarily mean they are "capable or conversant in a subject area." He added that to be successful at writing school science tests is not the same as thinking like a scientist: "The problem is that report cards rarely offer a reliable measure of what they appear to be reporting on."[11]

Mastery learning fits with apprenticeship experiences, where students begin as newcomers or novices, with the goal of becoming apprentices and possibly experts demonstrating more advanced levels of understanding. Stakeholders need to be aware that when COVID-19 influences the closure of schools and universities for safety purposes, there is a considerable impact on the social needs for learning.

Although virtual learning provides a different kind of social experience, it cannot replace the relationships at play in the classroom between the teacher and students and students with each other. Sellar (2021) noted that the closing of schools "created a 'glitch' in this critical social infrastructure that drew attention to aspects of education that were previously taken for granted."[12]

According to Green and Castanheira (2012), "individuals and the collective learn through interaction over time and, through this process, continually (re)formulate social, historical and cultural knowledge."[13] When social time is interrupted, it cannot be assumed that technology can manage the need for students to move back and forth between collective and individual learning experiences.

Vygotsky's (1978) work included the identification of the Zone of Proximal Development (ZPD),[14] whereby a novice learns to speak and behave like an expert through social interaction. When the novice, turned apprentice, no longer needs the aid or support of the expert, to demonstrate an understanding of a subject matter, one could say the student has achieved mastery.

To grasp the cultural know-how of an expert, novice learners need authentic social contexts for learning. As Dewey (1899) noted:

> From the standpoint of the child . . . the great waste in the school comes from his inability to utilize the experiences he gets outside of the school in any complete and free way within the school itself; while on the other hand, he is unable to apply in daily life what he is learning in school.[15]

Different from mastery, but similar, is the notion of experiential education, where students take part in a coop or internship, usually in a pre-career type of course. Such courses are typically not graded, but a portfolio of skills can be attained and documented. The idea of portfolio-based report cards seems to be a fresh wave for the future, sharing details of experience and what students have come to understand in the context of authentic and relevant work.

Criteria for portfolio report cards can be quite rigorous, while the qualifiers can vary, they can mirror traditional A, B, C, D rankings; a numerical 1–2–3–4system; a modified system (A, B, NY ["not yet"]); a pass-fail basis; or a gradeless, purely experiential assessment. Given the complexity of an experiential context, criterion-referenced assessment makes sense for guiding portfolio work and feedback.

In New Zealand, some teachers use a free e-portfolio service called My Portfolio (http://myportfolio.school.nz/), which "provides a personal learning environment to record and showcase evidence of achievement, manage development plans, set goals, and create online learning communities . . . Most New Zealand universities have introduced *MyPortfolio* to their teacher training programmes."[16] Furthermore, "the use of digital tools allows collecting information on student progress in a broader range of formats including text with hyperlinks, video, audio and simulations."[17]

Often extracurricular activities are evaluated as pass or fail; lifeguard qualifications, coaching certifications, first aid, and CPR all require an investment of time, and some with a minimum testing score to achieve the pass. There is no assurance that the lifeguard who scored 91% will be more capable of saving a drowning victim than a lifeguard who scored 89% on a required test for certification. Recently, experiential learning opportunities are offered in the form of micro-credentials. Further assessment options for micro-credentials are detailed in Chapter 5.

Probably the most nonsensical way of chunking reporting numbers happens when schools calculate grade point averages (GPA). At an expert roundtable in California, Douglas Reeves (2021) noted: "You can't say, 'I believe in social and emotional learning; I believe in resilience, in bouncing back,' and then turn around and use the average and say . . . 'I'm going to punish you today for mistakes you made three months ago.'"[18] The simplicity of doing mathematics to find a simple average score cannot address the reality of serious issues of mental illness and the direct links to school grades.

Prior to COVID-19, the number of young people who committed suicide was already alarming. After trying to adapt to lockdowns and the isolation during the pandemic, reports now indicate the number of teens with depression has doubled.

A parent at the roundtable shed light on anxiety in her own home when tears erupted over a grade dropping from an "A" to an "A-." Her disappointment described as "confidence-crushing defeat when hours of work and study fail to deliver an expected outcome." She added: "Even encouraging one-on-one communication with a teacher about a lesson or a grade can send my kids into a tailspin in ways I've not seen before."[19]

What makes this competitive culture more senseless is that people actually believe the system fairly ranks students. Bold administrators in the Northern Cass School District 97 decided to eliminate grade point averages and basically "blow up the system."[20] Author Yoree Koh (2021) wrote about how students "lacked the skills to make a mark on the world."[21]

To address student uncertainty about what to do with their lives after graduation, Superintendent Cory Steiner switched the district's emphasis from a traditional ranking focus to a competency-based education, "a form of personalized learning that emphasizes mastery of skills over time spent in class."[22]

If the way schools determine grades can be viewed as far from consistent, why then do schools use grades at all? Berkowitcz and Myers (2017) interviewed Thomas Guskey who admitted that there are some serious challenges with the way grades are determined. In the *EdWeek* article, it was noted that when assessment is used to sort and rank, "students see grades as scarce rewards offered to a select few rather than as recognition of learning success attainable by all." Doing well . . . means outdoing your classmates."[23]

Reporting with Teachers, Students, and Parents

A meaningful system for sharing student progress, beyond sending home a letter or numerical grade report card, requires schools to consider ideal ways for communicating feedback about student achievement and their habits for learning. The timing for teacher-parent conferences is often around 3–5 minutes with abrasive bells sounding the alarm to "move on." How can anything meaningful be discussed in such short time frames?

When the Jalen Rose Leadership Academy first opened its doors in Detroit, the school set aside a Saturday with 30-minute time slots for parent-teacher conferences. Having 94% parent turnout for the first semester conferences was telling. Even more convincing was the same turnout for the next series of meetings, as parents had a decent amount of time initially to talk, plan, and realize that their homeroom teacher really knew their child. Carving out significant time for such interactions should be the topic of more discussions about quality feedback opportunities in all schools.

What can be ironic is that parents, who are the furthest from the classroom learning context, tend to have these parent conference discussions without their children being present. Students have the most to gain, not simply by being there, but by addressing their work and setting goals for future learning. Having students present for at least part of an interview adds value. According to *EL Education,* "A student-led conference is a meeting with a student and his or her family and teachers during which the student shares his or her portfolio of work and discusses progress with family members."[24]

As a parent who has viewed student-led presentations, it was rewarding to hear my children speak with confidence about their learning. Absent from the encounter, however, was a sense from the teacher about their understanding of my child's learning during such student-led activities. Perhaps rethinking the idea of using the word "led" in feedback sessions is worthy of further thought.

The team at the nonprofit Common Ground Collaborative *(CGC)* organization see feedback as part of culture building. They recommend that schools use "curated learning conversations" where the teacher and the student discuss work together while inviting parent contributions as to their potential role in supporting the learning outside the classroom. In this way parents have a window into how the teacher interacts with their child, having access to these fishbowl-like discussions, leaving no mystery about next steps. Students do not enter curated conversations without a deeper understanding of self-assessment.

CGC promotes conceptual, competency, and character learning, "each with its own simple pedagogy and learning goals." According to the founding director, Kevin Bartlett, learning goals

> are expressed through agreed "sentence stems": *understand that, are able to, become more*, respectively . . . This clarity and simplicity supports learners in self assessing against "the 3 Cs" (conceptual, competency, character). This kind of systemic thinking holds great promise as we focus our attention on more relevant, authentic, personalised, student-led, qualitative approaches to assessment.[25]

Many school systems worldwide promote education as a winning and losing option.

As long as the goal is to rank students, schools have to accept the possible collateral damage that any child could be on the losing side of this game. Spear (2019) noted that senior educational leaders are aware of how much "the distortions of grading can get in the way of a genuine education,"[26] yet many systems continue to propagate assessment practices that educators know are not in the best interest of students.

Paying so much attention to test results assumes these data sources paint a relevant picture of what students truly know. Without assessing how well students apply what they know with others, in the contexts of classrooms, schools are only scraping the surface of what young people truly understand. To make matters worse, the high stakes tests aim to trick students, which adds to their confusion, frustration, and lack of respect for the process.

So, what fuels this love affair with testing? Even though administrators often demonstrate enthusiasm about changing the status quo, Spear suggests it is often short-lived as such initiatives are squashed by the perception that "parents will never go for it." He added: "As much as they may have wanted, in their secret hearts, to radically reconfigure their schools to deliver on the dream of a truly transformative education, they felt their hands were tied to stay with more conventional practices."[27]

Voices from within also convey myths that perpetuate sameness. "Don't change it, or other schools will not respect it," resonates from fixed mindsets unwilling to see the possibilities of improvement. The real estate of the report card is often a heavily guarded tool. The education (of parents and teachers), in concert with further research and ongoing documentation about the use of more progressive reporting tools, needs to be encouraged by leaders in education.

Families love their children unconditionally, and trust that school will be a safe haven for them to flourish, a place that will inspire and help them grow socially, emotionally, and physically, but intellectual diversity is not always accepted and celebrated. Even though teachers would not stand for their own professional evaluations to be subject to rankings, there seems to be little empathy for how much competitive swath is cast on students.

Parents pin high hopes and dreams that their child will be number one. It would be interesting to follow the trajectory of "top dogs," those who reign at the top of each class. How often do schools contribute to young people meeting their full potential? Is there a correlation between top of the class and work success? Many people think there must be a link, but where are the studies that provide some evidence that this may be so?

Examining carefully the words, letters, and numbers on the real estate of the report card can be a starting point for revising many outdated documents that can improve the kinds of feedback schools can provide for students and families.

Action Items

To move the dial forward on progressive reporting practices, school leaders and state/provincial/national education leaders need to consider several actions, such as:

- *Pause* the use of norm-referenced grading for ranking students.
- *Pause* (and remove) the use of medians on report cards for any that continue to exist.
- *Pause* the acceptance of Cs, Ds and Fs or related grades.
- *Pause* the use of grade 9 and 10 grades in GPA calculations.
- *Pause* the conditions for the uniformity of report cards.
- *Start* creating more criterion-referenced reporting tools that support learning.
- *Start* documenting and tracking relevant skill development and acquisition.
- *Start* using Not Yet as an indicator that students are not finished with the learning with a less than adequate grade.
- *Study* Carol Dweck's "Power of Yet" (https://www.youtube.com/watch?v=hiiEeMN7vbQ).
- *Study* how report cards contribute to learning.
- *Study* how criterion-referenced grading can align with authentic real-world experience recommendations.

To experience more progressive reporting practices, parents and teachers need to:

- *Pause* assumptions that the traditional report card is ideal.
- *Start* accepting the idea that there can be better ways of presenting feedback.
- *Study* how report cards can contribute to learning.

What would you like decision-makers to pause, start, or study?

NOTES

1. Kohn, A. (2019), https://www.alfiekohn.org/article/excellence/.
2. Ibid.
3. O'Connor, K. (2017), https://my.aasa.org/AASA/Resources/SAMag/2017/Jan17/OConnor.aspx.
4. Ibid.

5. Brookhart, S.M., Guskey, T. R., Bowers, A.J., McMillan, J.H., Smith, J.K., Smith, L.F., Stevens, M.T., & Welsh, M.E. (2016).

6. Ibid.

7. Ibid.

8. Ibid.

9. Ibid.

10. Macdonald, R. (2004), p. 86, https://www.plymouth.ac.uk/uploads/production/document/path/2/2434/Assessing_Enquiry_and__Problem_Based_Learning.pdf.

11. Spear, T. (2019), 130.

12. Sellar, S. (2021), 216.

13. Green, J., & Castanheira, M.L. (2012), 54.

14. Vygotsky, L. (1978).

15. Dewey, J. (1899/1998), 76–78.

16. OECD (2013), 188–189.

17. Ibid.

18. Reeves, D. (2021), https://edsource.org/2021/when-making-the-grade-takes-on-new-meaning/664591.

19. Ibid.

20. Koh, Y. (August 9, 2021), https://www.wsj.com/articles/how-schools-are-rewriting-the-rules-on-class-time-for-studentsand-even-ditching-grade-levels-11628517648.

21. Ibid.

22. Ibid.

23. Berkowitcz, J., & Myers, A. (September 7, 2017), https://www.edweek.org/leadership/opinion-dont-get-rid-of-grades-change-their-meaning-consequences/2017/09.

24. *EL Education,* https://eleducation.org/resources/chapter-5-student-led-conferences.

25. Bartlett, K. (2022), Email communication.

26. Ibid, 3.

27. Ibid.

4

Classroom Grading

What If?

WHAT IF TEACHERS DESIGNED THEIR OWN CLASSROOM ASSESSMENTS?

Assessment at the classroom level in the context of learning should be valued much more, and teachers who facilitate the context of the learning should play a key role in providing feedback and evaluating students. The OECD (2013) claimed that improvements in learning outcomes can happen when teachers and students engage with assessment information daily.[1]

Such engagement can happen on many levels. Teachers can talk about assessment tools with their students, but they can also prepare for learning by designing their own assessment tools, printing off prefabricated tools, or modifying existing tests and grading schemes from commercial materials or teachers past. Student input in the design or examination of existing assessment tools may also be encouraged. Regardless of the choice, there is much to discover about ways to assess students in classrooms.

Teachers who have the freedom and autonomy to generate assessment tools and reporting systems have distinct opportunities to choose what their expertise determines is the most appropriate metric for providing feedback to students and parents. Harvest Collegiate High School, for instance, "is part of a growing reform movement" that aims to place assessment "back in the hands of the people who work closest with students and their communities: teachers." At this school, students take part in "rigorous, teacher-created performance assessments" rather than state standardized tests.[2]

A license to design assessment should still be grounded in a solid understanding of current progressive practices in school assessment. Many teachers use commercial tests and rubrics developed by textbook writers because they trust the materials. A rubric can be defined as: "a scale that uses brief statements based on the criteria in the achievement chart and expressed in language meaningful to students to describe the levels of achievement of a process, product, or performance."[3]

School districts spend millions of dollars on commercial textbooks that include the accompaniment of prefabricated tests and assignment rubrics. Like standardized tests, these tools are often too wordy, repetitive, and lengthy. Often students do not have enough time to complete the tasks, as the expectations about the content to be taught make it difficult for teachers to provide ample time for learning.

The number of assignments handed out to cover curriculum content tends to be more about tasking rather than learning. Assessment tools, with built-in layers of assessment levels, enable teachers to teach a curriculum without the expectation that all students would master and learn with a deep level of understanding. Why else would a rubric go into depths about levels that do not meet mastery levels of understanding? If criteria for a qualifier such as "below expectations" exists, then it stands that the teacher can accept such levels of understanding, and move on.

A Not Yet, however, as a temporary metric, means the teaching, nor learning, is not over until the student reaches mastery. Educators should think carefully about the necessity for creating too many levels of achievement. The rubric should act as a guide to help students understand explicit expectations, in advance of their work. Why would anything less than a proficient level of understanding be accepted as completed work?

By collapsing everything less than proficient into a category called Not Yet, students and teachers can be encouraged to go back and improve upon work that has not met at least a mastery standard. Using the term Not Yet, as Carol Dweck[4] from Stanford suggests, relays a message that the work is not a degree of failure or inadequacy, but rather it represents a starter level of understanding that needs more work in order to achieve at a proficiency level.

The phrase "getting there" also offers a positive and more motivating message. The term "incomplete" has been used sometimes, but the emphasis is on what's missing, as opposed to the degree of understanding attained. The language of feedback matters, especially if educators see assessment as a tool for learning.

The 4H Club published an evaluation toolkit to help guide youth leaders for community change projects. One evaluation tool used three words as qualifiers, "awesome," "so-so," and "yuk," to differentiate how well they achieved specific criteria associated with making the ultimate chocolate chip cookie. While such qualifiers may not at first seem to be the most elegant vocabulary choices, their rubric did function to distinguish between three levels of taste.⁵ Even with three options, there can be inconsistent reviews as what is perceived as "so-so" and what is "yuk."

Rubrics used in school as a guide for an assignment or an assessment tool for a project need to have reliable qualifiers and clear criteria. The strongest rubrics should yield the same results from different users. Effective rubrics can include both formative and summative measures. According to Laveault and Allal (2016): "Information gathered on student learning may serve several different purposes, whether it is to *report on* student learning or *support* student learning, or both purposes at the same time."⁶

It is often reported that formative assessment relates to assessment for learning and summative assessment focuses on assessment of learning. However, as Laveault and Allal claim:

> Observation of classroom practice and discussions with teachers show that there is often a zone of overlap between the formative assessments they practice and seek to promote, and the summative assessments they are required to carry out by the school system.⁷

An English teacher may focus on many expectations in the process of writing at different stages. While the purpose of the feedback may be formative, it can also be summative when students demonstrate the capacity to edit their work in the formative stages of writing.

Good (2011) prefers to use the expression "formative use of assessment information"⁸ to identify the function of assessment. He added, "labeling an assessment item or activity as summative or formative without considering the timing and use can be misleading regardless of the quality of the item or the connection to instruction."⁹

Allal (2013) indicated that when determining a mathematics grade for a student's report card, "the teacher takes into account summative test results but also observations and discussions with the student during formative assessments integrated in mathematics workshops during the semester." She added: "This use of formative information is seen as making the final summative assessment more robust and valid than would be the case if the teacher simply calculated the average of the mathematics test scores."¹⁰

Later, Laveault & Allal (2016) recognized that "assessment activity includes phases or components with a formative function in support of learning, as well as phases or components with a summative function." In this way classroom activity can "foster student learning and at the same time contribute to reporting on student learning."¹¹ Assessment of learning relates to ranking students, whereas assessment for learning (AfL) focuses on what student's reveal about their own learning, without comparing scores to others.

Laveault and Allal noted: "It is a core principle of AfL that the evidence collected and used to make adjustments should benefit the students who provided the evidence."[12] Expectations should not be a mystery; the message of the rubric should not be cumbersome, with so many words repeated with added adjectives of "some" or "more" of a particular expectation. It can be difficult for students who should be using the tool as a guide to see the forest through the trees.

Carefully constructed assessment tools can be instructive. Teachers who hand out rubrics in advance of the assignment are demonstrating informed practice. Students can use the rubrics to plan, and then use them again to re-submit work, after teachers provide formative feedback along the way.

Ensuring that students have an opportunity to self-assess their work is also a part of a strong rubric. According to Adie, Willis, and Van der Kleij (2018): "A focus on student agency in assessment acknowledges students as actors who make choices, and whose actions shape assessment practices in both anticipated and unexpected ways."[13]

Similarly, the OECD (2013) advised: "Put the learner at the centre and build students' capacity to engage in their own assessment."[14] Wyatt Smith and Adie (2021) proposed that we need to develop "students' knowledge of how to evaluate or self-assess their own work against stated referents, and expertise in recognising quality and applying this in goal-setting and self-monitoring." They added: "Assessment is thus a process in which both teachers and students 'see' and 'use' criteria to inquire into and improve learning."[15]

By using a comprehensive assessment tool, the student can reflect on expectations as well as teacher feedback, in reference to the work at various stages of completion. Each criteria can serve as a lens to review the work for editing and revision purposes, ideally with teacher feedback to clarify expectations, if needed.

The notion of student regulation can be supported by the process of self-assessment. To this point, Allal (2010) noted:

> Learning environments need to be designed so that they . . . enhance the regulation of learning. This means the introduction of feedback at each stage of a learning activity, the use of questioning techniques that stimulate student reflection about alternative ways of carrying out a task, and the provisions of some degree of task differentiation to take into account learner interests and choices.[16]

When students self-assess their progress, they become more aware of expectations. Few textbooks provide tools with combined self and teacher assessment rubrics, yet the research about the benefits of self-examination are quite clear. Educators should not rely on osmosis, nor textbooks as curriculum to do the teaching and assessment tool construction; they need to trust their capacity and expertise in developing better tools that can shine a light on multiple evidence of learning.

When students are introduced to various rubrics, they often have to break down the expectations, especially when teachers use commercially designed tools. Removing the weeds can limit subjectivity, and help empower students to assess their own work, and use such tools as guides for following task directions. Take for example, the rubric in Table 4.1. It uses qualifiers of A, B, C, D, but you can also imagine such a rubric with a similar 1, 2, 3, 4 rating scale, as well.

Table 4.1 has some clear and useful criteria for measuring degrees of learning. It can be unwieldly when teachers hand students rubrics that are difficult to decipher. Keeping in mind that all rubrics can improve, here are some questions that can help educators examine rubrics with the goal of making customized materials to support classroom learning:

Table 4.1: Sample Writing Rubric from Thoughtco.com[17]

Areas of Assessment	A	B	C	D
Ideas	Presents ideas in an original manner	Presents ideas in a consistent manner	Ideas are too general	Ideas are vague or unclear
Organization	Strong and organized beg/mid/end	Organized beg/mid/end	Some organization; attempt at a beg/mid/end	No organization; lack beg/mid/end
Understanding	Writing shows strong understanding	Writing shows a clear understanding	Writing shows adequate understanding	Writing shows little understanding
Word Choice	Sophisticated use of nouns and verbs make the essay very informative	Nouns and verbs make essay informative	Needs more nouns and verbs	Little or no use of nouns and verbs
Sentence Structure	Sentence structure enhances meaning; flows throughout the piece	Sentence structure is evident; sentences mostly flow	Sentence structure is limited; sentences need to flow	No sense of sentence structure or flow
Mechanics	Few (if any) errors	Few errors	Several errors	Numerous errors

- How can all students and teachers distinguish between different qualifiers (i.e., "strong," "clear," and "adequate" levels of evidence)?
- How can rubric designers avoid combining different expectations within one cell (i.e., "originality" and "consistency"; "punctuation errors" and "grammatical errors"; "sophisticated nouns" and "weaker verbs")?

By describing the quality of less than a proficient (less than a B standard) level of achievement, it seems as if students have an option of producing ideas that are "too general" or some ideas that are "vague and unclear" in their written submissions. Now, consider doing a rubric makeover that includes an opportunity to self-review and fine-tune precise writing habits. Table 4.2 features an alternative *interactive rubric* designed to increase student engagement, reliability, and ease of use.

In this mastery-focused assessment approach, any score of less than 48 points would require the student to return to the writing piece and complete more edits until the work has met at least the identified proficient level. In the comment section, teachers should reference evidence of exceptional work and/or provide suggestions that would help students see how their writing could improve beyond the listed criteria.

Some teachers prefer to give students more chances by assigning additional work. Extra credit opportunities may seem like good intentions, but they give students permission to move on from incomplete work, something that in the real world would less likely be tolerated. Furthermore, there is no guarantee

Table 4.2. Sample Interactive Writing Rubric

Self-Review	2 = excellent level of evidence; 1 = some evidence; NY = Not Yet	Teacher Review
	Ideas presented in a logical manner (a nice flow)	
	Ideas include solid details	
	Ideas include original creative thought	
	Strong and organized beginning paragraph	
	Captivating starter sentence	
	Strong and organized middle paragraphs	
	Strong and organized ending paragraph	
	Inspiring/memorable ending sentence	
	Use of sophisticated nouns	
	Use of sophisticated verbs	
	Use of words and/or punctuation to transition sentences smoothly	
	Use of a variety of sentence types for emphasis	
	Accurate grammar	
	Accurate spelling	
	Accurate punctuation	
/30 points	Scores (Mastery 48 points or greater)	/30 points

that the quality of the next assignment will improve. Without attention to feedback in the context of the student's work, how can a student learn from their mistakes? It's like expecting skiers to improve their technique by doing additional runs down the slopes.

As teacher Gary Armida (2019) noted: "The idea of giving a redo is perhaps the single most misunderstood concept in education." He recognizes this is much more work for him, but he expects his students to redo assignments until they show mastery by "rewriting essays until they received the highest scores on the rubric in every area" and "looking at projects again, completing the elements that were missing. It includes redoing most assessments."[18]

Teachers who use rubrics for the purpose of recognizing strengths as well as identifying what's missing or what needs more work are making visible ways to increase the critical mass of mastery learners in their classrooms.

Rubric Makeovers

Do the steps taken to transform the rubric from Table 4.1 to Table 4.2 make sense? How do you think a parent might perceive each rubric? How much easier would it be for a teacher to tabulate a score using this revised tool? And finally, how well do you think the remodeled rubric could guide a student to success?

Textbooks can be used effectively as resources, but it makes sense for teachers to customize their own tests and rubrics to meet their student needs. Teacher may choose to revise existing rubrics. A makeover for shifting a conventional rubric to more of a tool for learning can happen with three easy steps that can simplify the volume of text for students and teachers to read, and use as a learning device:

1. Create three columns:
    i. one for the standard (written out once)
    ii. one for the self-assessment
    iii. one for the teacher criteria
2. Eliminate multiple standards lumped together.
3. Create a code for the qualifier of the standard.
      Note: People can distinguish with regularity evidence that:
    i. does not appear to be present
    ii. is somewhat present partially
    iii. meets the expectation fully

Educators need not assume that just because a rubric is part of a commercial package that it cannot improve. Any assessment tool can be adjusted to further support learning. Without a doubt, the Table 4.2 makeover sample can be improved, as well. Teachers who know what has been taught should be in the driver's seat to design and edit assessment tools to meet the needs of their students.

Feedback is at the core of learning. Assessment is not separate from curriculum; it's an integral part of it. According to the OECD (2013): "If the assessments do not match the curriculum and the standards, then assessment results have little value in judging how well students are learning."[19] So how does classroom assessment contribute to supporting more effective and motivated study? What is assessed within classrooms must be more than completed products. The process of getting to the end of the task matters, too.

Clarifying for students their need to talk with others about what they are learning is paramount in ideal classrooms. How often do parents receive feedback about the quality of student interactions during presentations, discussions, and other group or paired tasks? Why is it optional in many schools for students to write and share speeches?

The capacity to communicate in written and verbal forms is a relevant and necessary asset for future success. Table 4.3 features an interactive rubric designed to support positive discussion habits.

The capacity to communicate understandings is a significant employability skill, yet this aspect of learning in the realm of most subject areas is somewhat hit and miss. The pitch in *Shark Tank* can emerge from innovative curriculum combining elements of Junior Achievement[20] within Science courses, emphasizing communication for all students. All does not have to be quiet on the learning front.

Table 4.3: Sample Interactive Discussion Rubric

Self-Assessment	2 = excellent discussion habit; 1 = some evidence of good discussion habit; NY = good discussion habit not yet evident	Teacher Assessment
	Responded to questions with careful thought	
	Took notes that record the contribution of others in the discussion	
	Used notes/diagrams made during discussion	
	Asked questions in a whole class discussion that added to the conversation (no repeat ideas)	
	Waited for silence before making a contribution	
	Linked to other's ideas; responded with names of classmates	
	Expressed ideas in 2–3 sentences	
	Listened with an interested body look	
	Spoke with a respectful tone	
	Encouraged others to contribute to discussion	
/20 points	Total Score: /40 points	/20 points

Comments:

If talk is the closest thing to thought, then schools need to promote and assess much more talk, and support students in deliberate efforts to communicate their understandings beyond the pencil and paper test. Those dated schools, where you can hear a pin drop in the hall or in the classroom, need to become more aware of the inherent value of talk in learning.

The following sample (Table 4.4) adapted from Harvard's The Good Project illustrates three clear qualifiers for assessment, namely areas that "need work" (concerns), "meets standards," and "exceeding standards."

Table 4.5 adds self-assessment to adapt the tool in Table 4.4.

Customized rubrics can be different from the wordy boxed matrixes that can leave the assessment recipients overwhelmed with options. By removing the description of each qualifier, it can help students have an explicit understanding of expectations. Too many options for grading, such as the traditional A-B-C-D-F, or more popular 1–2–3–4 quadrant type options, are more subjective than the examples presented in Tables 4.2, 4.3, 4.4, and 4.5.

Not only can fewer grading options bring clarity, they can reduce subjectivity and increase reliability; teachers can come up with more aligned agreement on what constitutes proficiency, rather than wade into interpreting the degrees of "almost met" expectations, and what clearly "needs to be revisited and improved." It seems that making room for Cs, Ds, Fs or 1s and 2s just adds to widening of gaps that leave learning behind.

Teachers need to be front and center in the thick of assessment design. Schools need to help teachers find as many ways as possible to help all students learn. It would be so easy to print off some fun finds on Pinterest and Teachers-Pay-Teachers, but it would be wishful thinking to assume they precisely fit the teacher and students' needs. Teachers are not old dogs who cannot learn new tricks, by any means! They have fresh sharp minds that

Table 4.4: Adapted from The Good Project Rubric[21]

Concerns – Areas that Need Work	Meets Criteria – Standards for this Performance	Advanced – Evidence of Exceeding Standards
Criterion 1: Articulate the meaning of "good work" defined by excellence, ethics, and engagement		
Criterion 2: Differentiate and understand the relationship between "good work" and "work"		
Criterion 3: Identify and articulate the values that are most important to the student		
Criterion 4: Understand how school and other communities think of excellence, ethics, and engagement—or their absence		

Table 4.5: Adapted Assessment for The Good Project

Self-Assessment	C—Concerns—Areas that need work M—Meets Criteria—Standards for this Performance A—Advanced—Evidence of Exceeding Standards	Teacher Assessment
	Criterion 1: Articulate the meaning of "good work" defined by excellence, ethics, and engagement	
	Criterion 2: Differentiate and understand the relationship between "good work" and "work"	
	Criterion 3: Identify and articulate the values that are most important to the student	
	Criterion 4: Understand how school and other communities think of excellence, ethics, and engagement—or their absence	

Comments:

are more than capable of designing effective feedback and assessment tools. Systems that minimize preparation time for such innovation, resist change in education.

School administrators need to ensure that ample time is afforded for classroom rubric and test design. The teacher whose role is limited to "technician" will lift tests and rubrics off the Internet or photocopy them from teacher textbook guidebooks, but the "professional" teacher will use a design opportunity to collaborate and further develop tools to enhance student learning. The act of improving teaching and learning materials also contributes to furthering professional growth.

Schools need to give teachers permission to think out there. If lack of time is a factor in choosing less than adequate assessment tools, then the old dogs in the ivory towers need to make time to make the ideal happen. As Spear (2019) so elegantly claims: "Most of the really great things that happen in schools come about when individual teachers or learning assistants decide to put their own personal stamp on a program or process . . . ." He added:

> Much of the uninspired teaching and unbearable tedium . . . comes about when there is no motivation and support to do otherwise. One of our biggest challenges, therefore, is to give individual practitioners both the reasons and the structural support they need to do remarkable things with their students.[22]

Deliberately absent from these ideas for classroom grading is the notion of penalties for late work. In classrooms that teach content and "being on time" skills as a learned behavior should credit students for demonstrating such solid work habits. However, a score of 18/20 reduced to 60% because a student was deducted for lateness does not reflect what the student knows.

Ferriter (2021) questioned the value of penalties and stiff consequences. If they worked, "you would immediately see students changing their behavior in response to them," adding "kids would get one zero and then never miss another assignment."[23] Student who are struggling continue to do so, no matter what portion is deducted from the final score.

On his blog, Ferriter added: " . . . pretending like point penalties and rigid grading practices actually develop responsibility in students ignores reality. Those strategies just don't work—and clinging to them is the quickest way to prove that you aren't interested in acting professionally."[24] The practice of engineering ways of reducing scores for lateness qualifies hands-down as an assessment flaw.

Action Items

Ask teachers to pause, start, or study the following:

- *Pause* the impulse to take shortcuts; you are a capable and talented professional.
- *Pause* trusting one-size-fits-all rubrics and tests—developed by teachers or textbook writers who have not taught your students.
- *Pause* the practice of penalizing late assignments.
- *Start* gathering multiple forms of evidence of student learning.
- *Start* paying attention to how your students are applying their understandings.
- *Start* designing your own less wordy rubrics with embedded self-assessment options for students.
- *Study* notions of Backward Design (https://cft.vanderbilt.edu/guides-sub-pages/understanding-by-design/).
- Study (Follow) ASCD (http://www.ascd.org/); Canadian Assessment for Learning Institute (http://caflnforum.ca); specific subject-related associations (English, Math, Science, PHE . . .).

What do you think schools need to pause, start, or study with reference to classroom grading?

NOTES

1. OECD (2013), 217.
2. Troutman McCrann, J.R. (2018), https://www.ascd.org/el/articles/putting-assessment-back-in-the-hands-of-teachers.

3. Ontario Ministry of Education (2010), 153, http://www.edu.gov.on.ca/eng/policyfunding/growsuccess.pdf.

4. Dweck, C., https://www.youtube.com/watch?v=J-swZaKN2Ic.

5. 4H, https://4-h.org/wp-content/uploads/2016/02/Rural-Youth-Development-Youth-Leading-Community-Change-Evaluation-Toolkit-Color.pdf.

6. Laveault, D., & Allal, L. (2016), 7.

7. Ibid.

8. Good, R. (2011), 1, https://scholarworks.umass.edu/pare/vol16/iss1/3/?utm_source=scholarworks.umass.edu%2Fpare%2Fvol16%2Fiss1%2F3&utm_medium=PDF&utm_campaign=PDFCoverPages.

9. Ibid.

10. Allal, L. (2013), 8–9.

11. Ibid., 9.

12. Ibid., 15.

13. Adie, L E., Willis, J., & Van der Kleij, F.M. (2018), https://link.springer.com/article/10.1007/%2Fs13384-018-0262-2.

14. Ibid., 222.

15. Wyatt Smith, C. & Adie, L. (2021), 400.

16. Allal, L. (2010), 350, https://unige.ch/fapse/people/allal/doc/Allal2010.pdf.

17. Cox, J. (2020), https://www.thoughtco.com/essay-rubric-2081367.

18. Armida, G. (March 3, 2019), https://theteacherandtheadmin.com/2019/03/03/extra-credit-diminishes-everything-and-everyone/.

19. Ibid., 167.

20. Junior Achievement, https://en.wikipedia.org/wiki/Junior_Achievement.

21. Barendsen, L., Bither, C., Clark, S., Fischman, W., Gardner, H., McHugh, K., & Mucinskas, D. *The Good Project,* https://static1.squarespace.com/static/5c5b569c01232cccdc227b9c/t/60ca3500b0b3ae4fbe941f69/1623864590713/Good+Project+Lesson+Plans+-+fillable.pdf.

22. Spear, T. (2019), 11–12.

23. Ferriter, B. (December 30, 2021), https://buildingconfidentlearners.com/2021/12/punitive-grading-policies-dont-teach-kids-to-act-responsibly/.

24. Ibid.

5

Assessment of Portfolios, Experiential Learning, and Awarding Micro-credentials

What If?

WHAT IF THE ASSESSMENT OF PORTFOLIOS, EXPERIENTIAL LEARNING, AND THE AWARDING OF MICRO-CREDENTIALS WERE MORE WIDESPREAD?

The use of portfolios, the practice of experiential learning, and the awarding of micro-credentials are not as commonplace in schools around the world as education experts might expect. Such progressive practices are often cited as examples of bold curriculum design, yet the sustained implementation of them in K-12 schools can be met with resistance from academic decision-makers.

Experiential Learning

Experiential learning can happen inside and outside the school walls. The process of observation and gathering narrative accounts tends to be more commonplace in primary classrooms, even though such methods of gathering learning evidence could happen throughout one's schooled learning journey.

Atkinson (2012) defined pedagogical narration in its simplest form as: "recording through photos, video, or transcription the ordinary moments of children's play."[1] He claimed that examining the social context of the classroom requires a narrative tool "that allows us to reflect on the theories and strategies that children develop, the way social relationships are explored, and the constant process of learning, of 'making meaning' that children undertake."[2]

When students take part in field trips outside of school, they are encouraged to see the connections between what they are learning and how such learning is applied in the real world. Recent school closures as a result of COVID-19 have reduced the number of these experiences considerably. Virtual options, whereby students can view what it's like to be at the Smithsonian, the Louvre, or the Exploratorium in San Francisco, do provide some rich opportunities of the *Matrix*-kind. It is not, however, the same as being there. There is much to learn in such co-learning experiential opportunities with museum experts and each other.

Internships or "co-op" placements can have an incredible impact on student learning. The 3DE program promotes the transformation of high schools "to be more relevant, experiential, and authentically-connected to the complexities of the real world in order to more fully prepare today's students for the demands of tomorrow's economy."[3]

Four high schools implemented the 3DE program that "focused on expanding career diversity to improve alignment to the real world."[4] One hundred students and five partner companies took part in the pilot program in the 2017–18 school year. Junior Achievement reported: "Initial results indicate the higher-order thinking required through the eleventh-grade curriculum continues to build students' capacity as they push toward graduation."[5] Such findings speak to a shift in culture with clear gains in academic achievement.

At a Leonardo DaVinci-focused school in Virginia, students worked with their parents to create *family projects*. The quality of the products and collaborative effort generated work that was highly original. One term the families made their own planets, complete with river and governmental systems; another term they created their own community stamps and postcards; another term the student-parent teams created a mock 51st American state.

Each Leo Night that featured these projects was two hours in length. During the first hour, the students stayed at their table to present their projects, while the parents browsed the rest of the family creations; the second hour, the parents and students reversed their roles, so each student-parent partnership had an opportunity to present as well as view other projects. These creative works were gradeless, but represented many levels of expertise and learning. The families co-constructed their projects and together researched and created the evidence of what they learned in a collective product.

The discussion about the Leo Projects typically addressed the "how did you come up with these ideas?" which highlighted the valuing of the creative process. Participants exhibited many behaviors, most notably emulating what it's like to become an inventor and innovator. Being like Leonardo DaVinci was a community responsibility.

Even though this experience was not captured as a data point on the report card, it was nonetheless a powerful memory-making learning activity. How to facilitate these kinds of experiences in all kinds of schools remains a challenge, but such quality memories should not only be reserved for communities with deeper fiscal pockets and resources.

Project-based learning (PBL) is a popular experiential approach that can stand alone or be blended with mastery learning of government-regulated standards or other expectations deemed of value outside the traditional credit system. PBL is supposed to provide opportunities for students to make personal connections while conducting meaningful work.

At Inquiry Hub in Coquitlam, BC, the schedule, school size, and commitment to project-based learning is paramount: "About half of students' time is scheduled with standard classes, while the remainder is left unstructured, so that students can do coursework and have help pursuing what interests them."[6]

In Singapore, students take an interdisciplinary subject called Project Work "to draw knowledge and apply skills from across different subject domains." Students are required to create a project that fosters "collaborative learning through group work." Each student makes an oral presentation. Both the product and process are assessed via a written report, an oral presentation, and a group project file whereby "each group member submits three documents related to snapshots of the processes involved in the project."[7]

The River Literacy Project was developed when superintendent and adjunct professor John Puglisi, from California State University, Channel Islands and California Lutheran University, teamed up with Kris Machtmes of Ohio University and Judith Green, from the University of California, Santa Barbara. They designed a "transdisciplinary, inquiry-based learning project . . . to connect children, teachers, classrooms, schools, and communities from around the world," online. The question "How can we help the river find its way for the next 100 years?" guided the common purpose for inquiry.[8]

Technology educator and researcher Sugata Mitra, popular for inspiring the movie *Slumdog Millionaire*, suggests that schools move away from single exams as a measure of what students know. The oral testing for the PhD where students defend their positions on their own work that applies knowledge, has much merit. With reference to such a "perfect model" for assessment, he noted: "It doesn't matter how good the child is at physics or history because I know the child can pick up what he needs to know, when he needs to know it."[9]

The creation of new courses and assessment systems takes an incredible amount of energy, as there can be so many obstacles in the path of innovation. For such engaging courses to survive, there needs to be a planned sustainable time frame in place, beyond a few years.

Artist, scientist, and social entrepreneur Ethan Estess from Santa Cruz, California, uses trash washed up on beaches to tell stories with his sculptures to help viewers feel the disconnect between nature and humanity. His website features his work, which was inspired by his interdisciplinary program at Stanford: "I studied marine science while learning to express myself through sculpture. I balanced my study of ecology and oceanography with coursework in mechanical engineering and studio art."[10] His projects are stunning and steeped in social goodness.

The Buck Institute has compiled a number of resources that support the process for establishing a transformative learning environment. Its website claims: "Now more than ever, we need young people who are ready, willing, and able to tackle the challenges of their lives and the world they will inherit—and nothing prepares them better than Project Based Learning."[11]

Sustained inquiries, according to the Buck Institute, require students to take part in tasks that:

- have real-world relevance for learning;
- lead to deeper understanding and greater retention of content knowledge;
- enable them to interact with adults, businesses and organizations, and their community, which can develop career interests;
- can be transformative, giving them a sense of agency and purpose;
- support them to gain skills for today's workplace and in life (i.e., how to take initiative, work responsibly, solve problems, collaborate in teams, and communicate ideas);
- encourage teachers to work closely with them to support meaningful work, and share in the rediscovered joy of learning;
- help them enjoy a spectrum of technology tools for researching, collaborating, and presenting.[12]

Speaking of what students need, Berger (2012) noted: "They are not here to fill in the blanks on worksheets: they are here to accomplish original, beautiful work."[13] The Buck Institute goes as far as establishing a Gold Standard PBL model that includes doable and objective qualifiers. Students have either included "features of effective PBL," "features need further development," or "lacks features of effective PBL." The website suggests that educators "who are new to PBL, can see how to move from beginner to expert."[14]

Portfolios

When portfolios are used effectively, they can be powerful motivational tools for students. Portfolios are modified reporting tools that can document experiential learning. Cooperative experiences where students go into the community and work in various careers is also a difficult credit to simply capture with a percentage grade. Checklists, built into portfolios, can be used as a way of gathering learning evidence. Often portfolios work well with PBL approaches. Checklists can build in expectations as instructional guides for assignments and classroom tasks.

Portfolios not only clarify what needs to be mastered but also enable students to view progress over time. The idea of shifting to portfolios as a key reporting system can be met with trepidation, probably because there are limited examples of their sustained implementation. Unfortunately, many states and provinces in North America use standardized report cards, so the option of designing and using portfolios to replace traditional reports cards can be frowned upon, as it deviates from the norm.

Many educators and parents also assume that the use of portfolios means a gradeless or pass/fail evaluation process, without realizing that portfolios can also be made with qualifiers within rubrics to accent growth at various steps along the way.

Current reporting practices should continue to evolve. Spear (2019) acknowledged how easy it is for assessment in schools to "wag the dog." In *Education Re-Imagined: The Schools Our Children Need*, he noted that "we need to shift away from traditional report cards that offer rank order descriptions of student achievement within different subject areas and move toward a more sophisticated use of something like portfolios and individual learner profiles." He added: "We need to do this in a way that . . . reveals a broader range of understanding and ability than is typically embedded within a standard report card."[15]

At the Island Pacific School, Spear designed a "learner profile"[16] which promoted a variety of rich learning experiences that can be documented in portfolios. Spear's student profile unleashes the possibilities of how educators could coordinate portfolios of learning evidence. Students have much to learn from workshops or special courses.

In a 21st-century school, learning how to make a website or a computer app or apprenticing in special trades should not be considered nice options for a few students. External credentials for students could include first aid or babysitting certification, carpentry apprenticeship hours, or even a chainsaw safety training course. Student pianists, gymnasts, or chess masters could also be encouraged to document their experiences in portfolios.

What's required with all innovation is further education of outlying ideas so parents, teachers, students, and admission personnel can nurture the growth mindset required to embrace such powerful experiences and assessment tools. Even though many administrators and curriculum leaders are aware of the limitations of conventional assessment, there continues to be a concern about doing something that is different.

Often those who challenge such change may allege that portfolio use is experimental, noting that without massive implementation, it is an unproven choice. Every day, however, many employers in the world of work use qualitative evidence in the form of resume experience and work accomplishments to make decisions about whether some employees will be promoted or laid off.

The sheer authentic nature of the portfolio as a collection of evidence is a solid option that could and should be available to more students.

Micro-credentials

Given the relative newness of micro-credentials or nano-degrees, it makes sense that they may be defined in a few distinct ways. Colleges and universities tend to associate this credentialing process using experts in academic institutions, whereas industries tend to focus on their own in-house expertise. The Ontario government defines micro-credentials as "rapid training programs offered by colleges, universities and Indigenous Institutes across the province that can help you get the skills that employers need. They help people retrain and upgrade their skills to find new employment."[17]

Ontario Tech University identifies micro-credentials as evidence "created with industry, so you can be assured that the skills you are learning are in demand and current."[18] The current trend seems to focus on workplace skills; there, it is possible for any credential to be chunked into micro parts to support specialization of learning anything. As such, a micro-credential, defined as a "certification of assessed learning associated with a specific skill or competency,"[19] seems to provide more comprehensive options for students.

Achievement in the form of micro-credentials exists in community colleges and in many ways may have evolved from the idea of badges in the scouting system, swimming qualifications, or music conservatory grades. At school, student participation in extracurricular experiences such as band, team sports, intramurals, leadership, community service, and visual arts is often tracked through customized points systems that help to determine who gets school awards, activity or athletic letters. The NCAA recognizes athletes as "All American" for competing on varsity teams while achieving high academic grades.

Ideally, micro-credentials should include the criteria that was achieved on a mastery level, the listing of the qualifications of the accreditors, a document in digital or paper form, badge or certificate that indicates the time dedicated to the experience, as well as an expiration date, if required. Micro-credentials can be offered online or face-to-face with others at the same time, or on your own to fit a personalized schedule.

Mehta and Fine (2017) noted that "core disciplinary classes rarely afford students a glimpse into the domains to which they are connected." Recognizing the potency of extracurricular experiences, they noted links to apprenticeship learning. Unlike other school subjects, "adults who lead these activities frequently continue to be involved as participants as well as teachers—they play in adult soccer leagues, act in community theaters."[20]

The idea of cognitive apprenticeship enables learners to talk like and with, as well as behave like, experts. On the novice, apprentice, and expert scale, where would teachers be, or where might they see themselves on such a continuum?

Mehta and Fine (2017) claim that an athletic practice or theater rehearsal can create "an ethos that combines playfulness with purposefulness, drawing together the warm virtue of passion and interest with the cooler virtues of intellectual demand."[21] Given the value of such skills and understandings, it makes sense to consider such micro-experiences as cocurricular, enhancing their current status and therefore disrupting the conventional order of operation by expanding the notion of the Carnegie credit.

At the Island Pacific School, all students must complete a Masterworks class as a graduation requirement. Examples of grade 9 creative intellectual challenges include:

- The Many Worlds Interpretation in Quantum Mechanics
- Between the Lines (A Film Short)
- An Overview of Developed World Automobile Emissions
- Chad Is Making a Guitar!
- The Pressure to Be Perfect: Western Society's Approach to Body Image
- Is Euthanasia Morally Defensible?[22]

According to Spear (2019), it is important to structure supports for students in these Masterworks classes: "Each student has an advisory committee consisting of a teacher as the internal chair and one or two External Faculty who are adult volunteers outside the school with an interest in the topic being investigated."[23] Often innovative programming requires an examination of the effectiveness of supports. Giving students an opportunity to speak with and like experts can expand the apprenticeship capacity of individual student pursuits.

At the Moanalua Middle School in Honolulu, Hawaii, Robert Walker, a 34-year-teaching veteran, transformed his practice when he began to introduce robotics into his industrial arts classes. Some examples of their creations included mechanical chopsticks, automated car washing, and frisbee-throwing machines. Some of their work even outperformed robots built at Stanford and Cornell. One student commented that the process was like "turning your imagination in reality."[24]

At the Brown Deer School, technology/shops teacher Craig Griffie coordinated the "Building2Learn" program where private, public, and charter schools have programming inside local construction and manufacturing companies. Students who enroll in Griffie's Pre-Apprenticeship Readiness Program come to school early to gain practical experience "working with tools and their hands."[25] While no credits or grades were awarded, students who completed the program received a certificate "knocking 500 hours off the requirements for a carpenter's apprenticeship."[26]

Griffie was eventually recruited to work in Brookfield, Wisconsin, as part of the LAUNCH Program, which featured a host of authentic learning options. The website outlines how LAUNCH is a collaborative of education, business, and community members who provide students with a "unique, immersive experience, resulting in highly skilled, adaptable, global innovators and leaders."[27]

Experiential learning options included:

- Data Science & Intelligence for Careers
- Law & Public Policy
- Skilled Building Trades
- Advanced Manufacturing & Design
- Biomedical Solutions
- Business Analytics
- Foundations of Body Systems & Disease
- Future Teachers
- Global Business
- Engineering Foundations
- Hospitality Innovation

These courses are hosted at one of four schools in the community that share the local resources and human capital.

Each option could be used as micro-sections of credits. For instance, "Law & Public Policy" is a three-credit course broken down into:

- AP Language and Composition (1 credit)
- Current Issues (0.5 credit)
- Crime, Society, and Law (0.5 credit)
- Mentorship (1 credit)[28]

Authorities who granted the carving up of Carnegie credits into more manageable and relevant areas of study were demonstrating not only a growth mindset, but impressive insight into experiences that bring about student engagement.

What is compelling about these courses is that they reach across dated assumptions that the practical arts are less rigorous than other more traditional course work. Students who want a career in construction, carpentry, or plumbing, for instance, can benefit from certification in the building trades, but students seeking other careers can also have access to learning skills from various hands-on trades. The arbitrary separation of careers and academic standards can, as in real life, be less of a Grand Canyon to cross.

There are many commercial and industrial applications of micro-credentials. Boaters can take a course mixed with a test that certifies qualifications for driving a boat. People can take a course on YouTube that can teach and test one's capacity to operate a chain saw. IBM offers a series of Open Badges that move through "Explorer," "Advocate," "Inventor," "Certified," and "Excellence" qualifiers that describe various levels of competencies.

My Music Masterclass (MMMC) features an interactive experience with world-class artists who endorse music mastery. On this website they provide course material and instructions for students to film a video of themselves "performing the required musical tasks." They noted, "the artist watches this video and decides if the student has fulfilled the specified criteria outlined in the course."[29] Such opportunities provide students, not ready for mastery, with more time to learn and improve, noting "If the student doesn't pass, he or she will be told exactly what went wrong . . . and hopefully pass the certification at a later date."[30]

In the past, schools had to rely on their own human capital in order to provide varied programs to promote creative course offerings. Now with online courses developed for any virtual portal, schools can provide students with micro-credentials on a much wider scale. For over three decades, the Disney Institute[31] has been providing workshops and summits to share the "Disney Way" with people interested in renewing or refreshing their business practices. In the past decade, there have been many new micro-credential options that many young people are using as a boost for their resumes.

Skillshare offers 2,512 micro-courses that include learning options from a widespread of potential interests, such as:

- Art Journaling for Self-Care: 3 Exercises for Reflection and Growth
- Adobe Photoshop CC—Essentials Training Course
- Stock Market Fundamentals
- Spanish for Beginners. The Complete Method. Level 1.
- Photography Essentials: Understanding the Basics
- Basic Skills / Getting Started with Drawing[32]

Ernst & Young (EY) have embraced the use of digital badges across their professional network. Employees who complete 20 hours can earn digital badges, as well. They noted: "Since launching its EY Badges program in November of 2017, nearly 4,300 badges have been earned globally." The experience entails the passing of a simulated case study, a written synopsis "using specific tools in client situations," and "participating in relevant nonprofit work (i.e., *Girls Who Code* volunteering), or demonstrating digital industry experience (within the last two years), among other options."[33]

When browsing the Internet there seems like endless pages of opportunities, making it somewhat of a challenge to know which experiences might be worthy of dedicated time. Those associated with colleges and universities or those backed by professional associations seem to be more reliable sources; however, there are for-profit agencies that do provide unique quality experiences (i.e., the Disney Institute), while others may not.

McGraw-Hill is one of the first publishing companies to formalize chunks of coursework into micro-credentials. Color-coded "belts" are earned when students master Microsoft Office skills, noting they "can then post these digital certificates . . . through social media and add them to their resumes to showcase their accomplishments and reach the employers who have available positions."[34] McGraw-Hill responded to the need to increase student engagement in colleges. And as such, community colleges have been proactive to embrace and integrate micro-credentials for middle and high school-aged students as well.

As innovative practices in teaching and learning continue to evolve, so too can assessment practices. Indeed, if assessment is part of curriculum, it needs to develop in concert with new practices. Further research into the impact of portfolios, experiential learning, and micro-credentials needs to be front and center in how future schools evolve and continuously improve.

Actions Items

- *Pause* thinking that practical arts should be separate from the arts and science of academia.
- *Pause* thinking that apprenticeship learning is not rigorous.
- *Pause* saying there is no room or time in the curriculum for experiential learning.
- *Start* learning about the value of portfolios.
- *Start* recognizing the value of project-based learning.
- *Start* reviewing vitual museums and learning centers (i.e.,
- Smithsonian, https://www.si.edu/dashboard/virtual-smithsonian;
- Louvre, https://www.louvre.fr/en/online-tours;
- Exploratorium, https://www.exploratorium.edu/visit/virtual-tour).

- *Start* re-organizing courses to chunk material for deeper learning and assessment.
- *Start* accepting practical experiences and qualifications as evidence of learning.
- *Study* qualitative research to gain insight into rich experiential learning experiences.
- *Study* education websites such as MindShift (https://www.facebook.com/MindShift.KQED/).

There are many options for specialized courses and micro-credentials including:

- https://www.outlier.org/
- https://www.futurelearn.com/programs
- https://makered.org/professional-development/maker-educator-micro-credentials/
- https://www.wsps.ca/Shop/Tra`ining/Certification-Training-Overview
- https://outschool.com/classes

What do you think schools can pause, start, or study to make room for innovative practice?

NOTES

1. Atkinson, K. (2012), (http://www.jbccs.org/uploads/1/8/6/0/18606224/pedagogical_narration.pdf). Junior Achievement (2017),
2. Ibid.
3. https://www.atlantapublicschools.us/cms/lib/GA01000924/Centricity/Domain/11340/3DE%20Resources.pdf.
4. Ibid.
5. Ibid.
6. http://www.inquiryhub.org.
7. OECD (2013), 184.
8. Puglisi, J., Machtmes, K., & Green, J. *The River Project*, https://sites.google.com/rioschools.org/river-literacy-project/home/about?authuser=0.
9. Moreton, J. (April 2021), https://www.tes.com/magazine/teaching-learning/secondary/sugata-mitra-phd-style-vivas-should-replace-exams.
10. Estess, E. http://www.ethanestess.com/statement.html.
11. The Buck Institute, https://www.pblworks.org/why-project-based-learning.
12. Ibid.
13. Berger, R. (2012), http://68.77.48.18/RandD/Deeper%20Learning/Beautiful%20Work%20-%20Berger.pdf.

14. Ibid.
15. Spear, T. (2019), 136.
16. Ibid., 138–139.
17. https://www.ontario.ca/page/micro-credentials-ontarios-postsecondary-schools.
18. https://ontariotechu.ca/microcredentials/what-are-microcredentials/index.php.
19. https://www.ryerson.ca/diversity/news-events/2021/03/new-report-analyzes-canadas-micro-credential-trends-and-knowledge/.
20. Mehta, J., & Fine, S. (2017), https://www.gse.harvard.edu/news/ed/17/01/why-periphery-often-more-powerful-core.
21. Ibid.
22. Spear, T. (2019), 53.
23. Ibid.
24. https://www.hawaiinewsnow.com/2019/03/09/his-middle-school-robotics-class-imagination-is-just-important-math/.
25. https://www.building2learn.org/brown-deer-schools-tech-ed-teacher-craig-griffie-knocks-down-barriers-to-working-in-trades-daily-reporter/.
26. https://launch.yourcapsnetwork.org/about/.
27. https://launch.yourcapsnetwork.org/strands/.
28. Ibid.
29. https://www.mymusicmasterclass.com/product-category/get-certified-micro-credentials/.
30. Ibid.
31. https://www.disneyinstitute.com.
32. https://www.skillshare.com.
33. McCrea, B. (Spring, 2019), https://www.icpas.org/information/copy-desk/insight/article/spring-2019/leveling-up-your-accounting-and-finance-credentials.
34. https://www.mheducation.com/news-media/press-releases/mcgraw-hill-offers-simnet-credentialing-program-to-college-students.html.

6

Top Dog

What If?

WHAT IF RANKING STUDENTS DIDN'T MATTER?

When many parents send their kids to school, they hope to see their child as the "top dog," in other words, at the top of their class. What if schools did not use assessment to rank students? Would teaching and learning grind to a halt? Would more students feel successful in school?

Daniel Pink's book *Drive* explored new perspectives on what motivates people to be passionate about what they do, to be driven intrinsically, as opposed to responding to the carrots of extrinsic grades. Such lessons intended for business also apply to education. The website Pink Time warns that students who are primarily motivated by grades may forgo "a deeper engagement with the material and the learning process." Furthermore, students can be guided to "inspire themselves" and "engage more deeply in learning" when extrinsic motivation is stripped away leaving "more space for autonomy, mastery, and purpose."[1]

Why does it seem more important for policy makers to rank students rather than increase the critical mass of learners? If there is only one "top dog," in a class of 100, there are 99 others who missed out on being "number 1." The efforts to engineer such ranking systems, do not contribute to any sense of mass motivation; in fact, it might be fair to assume that the limited spaces for the top position do more to de-motivate students than not. Furthermore, how do educators know for sure that any assessment gets the rank ordering right? Many might assume the grading tools used in schools lead to an accurate arrangement of standings.

Without paying attention to peer-reviewed research that should support such claims, schools can continue to cultivate a competitive culture, without the use of expert tools to confirm such rankings. It is rare for anyone to question the selection of the "top dogs," so the practice of ranking students continues, as usual, in most North America high schools today.

Many materials used in schools have changed over the past century, and so have some tools used to select the "top dogs." New technology has also made it easier for schools to increase the volume of standardized testing. Has the increase in tests and practice tests enabled schools to make more precise ranking decisions, or just ones that feature more tired and stressed students? Being the "top dog" may be rewarding, but what is the impact of the ranking process on the rest of the student population? And, how healthy is it for students to be thrust into a competition to be the "top dog?"

Reflecting on the recent concerns surrounding the impact of COVID-19 on college admissions, one California parent shared:

> It's hard as a parent to stay true to your word about grades when you know California's college admissions stack your children against their peers—not just those in the state but the ones they sit next to in class. A huge shortage of seats at California's public four-year institutions has made applying for college feel like a scene from the "Hunger Games."[2]

In spite of the fact that standardized tests have been popular ranking tools for entry into most US universities, such tools function to carve students into three basic categories:

- students at or near the top of their class
- students in the middle of the pack
- a good chunk of students "checking out" at the bottom

Without being in the top third of test-takers, two-thirds of learners can be typically overlooked by college admission teams, missing a more comprehensive picture of the applicant.

This ranking story is like the *Twilight Zone* episode[3] where the character keeps dreaming about arriving at the same train station over and over. Students with the highest scores are usually accepted by universities with the highest rankings, and the pattern repeats itself year after year. Such a system is well received by students fielding higher SAT and ACT scores and 4.0 GPAs. Their parents tend to be very satisfied with this system of education echoing solid support: "It's working for us."

Many parents of high achievers have played the game, survived, and, in their worldview, have earned the right to keep the game rules intact. Some students who come from less affluent zip codes can often feel the strain, but may not care if the system is rigged or fair; they just want to "get out."

Educators cannot assume the sounds of silence are riveting rounds of applause for the current system. Surely, there are voices of discontent? After all, North Americans live in a democracy, where the dream should be accessible to all?

The message about "top dogs" and stars seems all about making a few students shine, with the light shining brighter from a contrast between winners and losers. Sadly, it seems that more winners might dim the brightness of the few "top dogs." Such a dated notion of winning seems to be augmented by the shadows of a significant number of students left in the dark.

Setting up students to compete against one another for a limited number of top grades on a report card continues to be commonplace in many schools. Hear the misinformed calls for rigor now: "The world is a grind." "We need to teach young people how to survive in the dog-eat-dog world."

It doesn't have to be this way. There should be opportunities for students to demonstrate their passions that may be distinct from their classmates, but there should be plenty of experiences where everyone wins, that is, all students learn to a proficient degree what is offered and created in the context of the curriculum. And it can be fun. What matters first and foremost was forming relationships, and after that students can begin to look at school through a different lens, one much more sophisticated than a narrow path of testing to feed the ego of a "top dog."

Actions Items

Ask parents if they can pause, start, or study the following:

- *Pause* pressuring students to get "all As" or be at the top of the class.
- *Pause* believing career choices should be based on test scores.
- *Pause* believing there are no second chances.
- *Start* learning about the value of mastery-based reporting practices.
- *Start* recognizing the value of project-based learning, internships, and portfolios.

Ask university admission directors if they can pause, start, or study the following:

- *Pause* the "all As" ceiling for admitting students.
- *Pause* elevated weightings of standardized scores (and publishing of ranges on college websites).
- *Pause* encouraging students to rewrite SATs and ACTs.
- *Start* using only 11th and 12th grades in a GPA.
- *Start* interviewing more students for admission consideration.

- *Start* learning about the value of mastery-based reporting practices and portfolio work.
- Start really paying attention to extracurricular, volunteer, and internship experiences.
- *Study* (Follow) https://www.facebook.com/groups/standardsbasedlearningandgrading/.
- *Study* for a graduate degree in education to access expert peer-reviewed research into assessment practices.

What do you think schools need to pause, start, or study?

NOTES

1. https://www.pinktime.org/about.
2. Vasquez, A. (December 19, 2021), https://edsource.org/2021/when-making-the-grade-takes-on-new-meaning/664591.
3. https://en.wikipedia.org/wiki/A_Stop_at_Willoughby.

7

Underdogs

What If?

WHAT IF ALL STUDENTS WERE EXPECTED TO MASTER WHAT WAS BEING TAUGHT?

Assessments that rank students invariably support the practice of identifying underdogs. The notion of building a critical mass of a knowing society cannot be about ranking, but rather more about mastery learning. The goal of helping all students master learning means that more people in life and the world of work will know things and be able to do more things to contribute to society. How can this be a bad thing?

As long as educators hold on to the idea of sameness, underdogs will be part of the collateral damage of education. While teachers understand the value of meeting students where they are, they can still use many resources and assessments that run counter to this ideal. Teachers need to embrace differentiation to plan for individualized needs. To get to the root of these needs, students should take a more active role, as majority stakeholders, in their education; test-makers and researchers should include the voices of the test-takers so such tools can evolve and have a more potent influence on learning, rather than *of* learning.

The idea that all students begin at the same starting block as their classmates seems hollow. Everyone learns at a different pace, regardless of their age, gender, socioeconomic status, or pedigree. How can educators assume that test scores and assignment grades have been assessed on a fair playing field? To make a scientific conclusion, schools need to be able to remove the variables that are not constant.

The underdog students bring all sorts of differences that affect their capacity to learn and demonstrate such understandings on tests and assignments.

By focusing on students, this chapter examines many barriers to learning, and how they cannot be ignored when comparing one student with another.

Students who do not test well often feel like underdogs: lonely, lost, and hopeless. They need a thunder-vest of caring teachers who believe in them. Without teacher support to help them fully succeed, they become the departed, learners who have left the building. Their bodies may be legally confined to desks, but their minds have moved on. Many embrace the learning channels of the World-Wide Web. As the legendary educator and mentor David Booth once said: "So many young people are building tunnels under their teachers and classrooms." Classrooms need to be safe spaces where young people learn with others.

Not only are too many students caught in a learning fog, too many teachers, administrators, and systems can be left lifeless, as well, absorbed by disconnected standards. How can the world of work link with internship experiences for all students? How can schools ensure all students learn robotics and chess? How can schools promote programs like Model United Nations[1] as authentic integrated units within history classes? All students can experience such powerful learning simulations, not just a few who sign up for an after-school club.

Not only must educators pay attention to what makes schools boring, teachers also need to step back and think about the uneasy relationship between compliant behavior and good grades. The more practices are standardized and regulated, the more students and educators lose opportunities to shape the future.

Seasoned educators or parents may recall watching *The Outer Limits* in the sixties. The introduction to each segment began with this narrative:

> There is nothing wrong with your television set. Do not attempt to adjust the picture. We are controlling transmission . . . We will control the horizontal. We will control the vertical. We can roll the image, make it flutter . . . For the next hour, sit quietly and we will control all that you see and hear. We repeat: There is nothing wrong with your television set. You are about to participate in a great adventure. You are about to experience the awe and mystery which reaches from the inner mind to . . . The Outer Limits.[2]

Test-makers, in a way, are controlling much of what is seen and experienced in many schools, and the reviews are not a great. It's not natural for students to be inactive learners. It can be a grueling lesson in patience when these underdogs have to "stay put" while the teacher at the front of the room explains the objectives for the whole class, demonstrates a few examples of the content or skills to be learned, then follows up with seatwork from a textbook or a prefabricated worksheet, and, for the last five or ten minutes, some Q and A.

While there is no evidence that such instructional approaches contribute to higher achievement, there is growing speculation that boring lessons lead to disengagement and behavior problems in classrooms. Furthermore, assessment choices may contribute to disengagement and inequity. According to the OECD (2013), "assessments that are not well designed and implemented may in fact contribute to alienating students (and teachers) from the education system and exacerbate inequity in education."[3]

Referring to teaching in higher education, Biggs and Tang (2011) addressed the practice of backwashing as disengaging, the antithesis of deep learning: "We teachers might see the intended learning outcomes as the central pillar in an aligned teaching system, but our students see otherwise." Backwashing happens when "students learn what they think they will be tested on." They suggested that this can include students going through previous papers to search out questions and "rote learning answers to them."[4]

Biggs and Tang claim that "this sort of backwash leads inevitably to surface learning."[5] Paying attention to what students say about school and actively pursuing their feedback could be illuminating. More than thirty years ago, Fullan (1991) begged the question: "What would happen if we treated the student as someone whose opinion mattered . . . ?"[6]

Committed to expanding the depth and breadth of cognitive skills in today's schools, Lucas and Claxton (2009) suggested: "Though the content of lessons has varied over the years, pedagogy has seemed designed, for a great many students, to cultivate a rather narrow set of cognitive skills and attitudes." Samples of narrow focus skills include:

- The ability to accept what you are told without question.
- Learning how to compute without understanding what you are doing.
- Copying notes quickly and accurately.
- Retrieving and transcribing information acquired months or years previously quickly and accurately.
- "Parking" your own mental and emotional concerns for large periods of your waking day.
- "Reading" teachers' minds.
- Sitting still for protracted periods of time.[7]

Based on an extensive review of assessment practices in many countries, the OECD (2013) reported concerns from stakeholders that assessment practices appear to "lag behind" informed approaches to teaching and learning: "Both national assessments and classroom-based assessments in many countries have remained focussed primarily on reproducing knowledge and applying basic skills, with less attention being paid to measuring complex competencies."[8]

Engagement loss in school is a serious concern. Behavior problems could be related to poor assessment practices and the volume of content they are expected to absorb. According to the OECD (2013), "the exponential rise in access to information has made it less important for learners to be able to recall and reproduce facts," adding that it is necessary to develop competencies that "synthesise, transform and apply learning in real-world situations, think creatively and critically, collaborate with others, communicate effectively and adapt to rapidly developing environments."[9]

Even though experts have been clear about the need for deep thinking, there seems to be fewer opportunities to think freely and creatively. The underdog voices, in particular, who were once vibrant and enthusiastic, can be muted by the overfeeding of facts and the tighter bonding of compliant behavior.

It's important to teach young people how to respect others and their surroundings. However, with the advent of testing and testing practice in schools, the notion of discipline in schools has taken on new meaning. In fact, the apparent need to train teachers in the art of making students obedient has been the source of some of the worst curriculum and instructional training witnessed by many in the past thirty years.

Many educators return to teaching basics, metaphorically expect students to "heel" on command, as if the classroom travelled back in time to Nazi Germany control in WWII. Such classrooms where students sit in individual desks, raising their hands on cue to spew out single words answers, never speaking without permission, does not mirror the cultivation of an innovative and inventive society. The teacher control of a classroom is anti-learning. The teacher is the alpha dog and all students, underdogs, in their subservient roles.

When a discipline issue arises, teachers need to find out what is at the source of the behavior, not simply click their fingers and signal the student, like a dog, to "sit." Identifying consequences can be a deterrent, but a narrow reactionary stance is not enough to address the complexity of the problem. Some schools call their rules "codes of conduct"; other terms such as "learning agreements" or "norms" can be more appealing to proactive stances. If students have codes of conduct, then it makes sense that teachers and parents should have them, as well.

All stakeholders need to respect school norms. When preparing agreements and norms for adults in a school building, the punchy language (i.e., "You are forbidden . . . ") used for students is often softened. Norms, ideally written with input from students, staff, and family members, can support positive behaviors. Rather than highlight a list of negative actions, such as being disrespectful or harming others, it is possible to promote expected character-building behaviors. All stakeholders can sign agreements indicating they agree to respect each norm.

Principals can play a role in teaching and implementing school norms. When stakeholders stray from the norms, the school leader can meet with them and discuss the value of the broken promise and consequences. They might then move forward with a newly signed agreement. Such agreements can be part of the student admission process, as well.

Being committed to reducing disrespectful and harmful behavior at all levels, at the same time as looking at what can be controlled in terms of providing more engaging learning contexts, is a practical way to change culture. The agreement itself is a feedback tool that can contribute to supporting positive school change.

The underdogs in classrooms can often project their frustration for missing out on learning by making their pitch to change the agenda in the classroom;,that is, through misbehavior. Relying only on agreements with recognized consequences, does not address the need for the underdogs to feel confident about learning.

Teachers need to see where gaps are, not only in communicating expectations, but how skills and understandings are broken down. They need to learn how to make the complex simple and how assessment can help support the learning process. Think about teaching writing. How often do teachers make students write daily, as if the more they write, the better they will get. Time out. The more someone writes, the more they can entrench poor practice. It's not enough to trust the activity in a textbook; great teaching usually requires further thinking, planning, and customized instruction.

Curriculum that links to student experience can be much more engaging than a one-size-fits-all textbook. Exceptional teachers integrate people, places and things from their local community. Too many teachers assume that if you followed the steps in the textbook, it must be the student's fault for not getting it. Wrong. Some people blame the teacher when students do not succeed. Wrong. Schools need to examine widespread patterns to see if systemic operations and expectations could be contributing to reducing the critical mass of student learners.

Educators can also do much more in schools with students who learn differently. Schools emphasize inclusion as a key way to support students with special needs, but just because they enter the air space of a classroom does not mean they are included. There are students who thrive in teacher-directed environments, some who tolerate them, and others who feel repelled by them. When the norms of such classrooms resonate around themes of compliance, that is, simply doing what you are told to do, then many students, not just those identified with special needs, will not feel included.

All students have better chances of engaging in an inclusive environment when they can participate in student-directed learning activities. Students are empowered when they have a sense of control. Furthermore, they feel a part of something when their uniqueness is accepted. It's not enough to simply place students in a classroom; all students need the opportunity to build capacity in a space that is safe, inspiring, and fun.

The idea that all students of a given age come equipped with the same physical, emotional, social, and intellectual capacity is a real misconception that can be addressed by alternative school structures. Naïve test-makers believe they are generating a true representation of bright student rankings at the top, and the weakest at the bottom, but what is affirmed is the fact that all students in a single grade are not the same. Yet, schools continue to organize based on age. When a test date for all looms in the spring, the talk (and action) tends to cheapen the claim that differentiated instruction is common practice.

How often do students have opportunities to take diagnostic quizzes at the beginning of a unit to determine what they already know or need to know. In a research-informed school world, this would be standard practice. Those who already know something should simply move on to a different task, but in the one-size-fits-all school setting, students must face the same music that anyone born in the same year must endure.

Even though multi-age classrooms can make differentiated teaching and learning possible, they are often frowned upon by teachers and parents. Not to be confused with split classes, where a teacher struggles to teach two completely separate curriculums at the same time, multi-age learning uses the same context, with multiple outcomes (enriched or remedial) that students can target.

It is easier for all underdogs to fit into multi-age classrooms, as they can work at their own pace, without social boundaries being implanted within conventional arbitrary age-based divisions school call grades. The myths that older students are held back are unproven, so it remains a challenge to educate all stakeholders about the value of such a learning context.

There are some strong similarities between teachers, leaders, and coaches. A coach may believe a team is only as strong as its weakest players. Likewise, a society may only be as strong as its weakest learners. Yes, schools need to provide a stimulating setting for the brightest in the bunch; it could be argued, however, that the cards are currently stacked in their favor already.

How can the test-makers actually believe they have a solid fix on student learning, when there are so many barriers at play? The path forward to a better way of assessment should pay attention to the test-taker, and more specifically the underdog's responses. Such messages should influence and inform the curriculum, not only what and how something is taught, but how that something is assessed. Educators need to recognize that the underdogs can always be our teachers, if only their voices are taken seriously.

Action Items

Ask students if they pause, start, or study the following:

- *Pause* believing that career choice should be based on test scores.
- *Pause* believing there are no second chances.
- *Start* questioning the use of wordy rubrics and subjective assessment tools.
- Start collaborating and supporting others to enhance learning.
- *Study* (Follow) https://www.facebook.com/groups/standardsbasedlearningandgrading/.
- Study (Follow) https://www.nasponline.org.
- *Study,* but make time for play.

What do you think schools need to pause, start, or study to support all learners?

NOTES

1. Model United Nations, https://www.un.org/en/mun/model-un-guide.
2. Outer Limits, https://en.wikipedia.org/wiki/The_Outer_Limits_(1963_TV_series).
3. OECD (2013), 145.
4. Biggs, J., & Tang, C. (2011), 197
5. Ibid.
6. Fullan. M. (1991), 170.
7. Lucas, B., & Claxton, G. (August, 2009), 9.
8. OECD (2013),149.
9. Ibid., 147..

8

Cycles of Teacher Feedback, Performance Reviews, and Professional Growth

What If?

WHAT IF TEACHERS ENGAGED IN CYCLES OF FEEDBACK, PERFORMANCE REVIEWS, AND PROFESSIONAL GROWTH?

Given that teachers can have such a significant impact on students and, subsequently, a school, it's important to provide a meaningful feedback system, performance review process, and professional growth activities that can help these educators grow and succeed in their jobs. Strong teachers are critical to a school's success. To support the goal of obtaining a substantial critical mass of "exceptional teachers," schools need all staff members to take part in a robust growth cycle that can be addressed over the course of a teacher's career.

According to Wiliam and Leahy (2014): "Teachers don't lack knowledge. What they lack is support in working out how to integrate these ideas into their daily practice, and this takes time, which is why we have to allow teachers to take small steps."[1] The Dylan Wiliam Center offers detailed planning opportunities for educators. Their action planning process "is best done with a highly structured approach—very different from the tokenistic "action planning" that occurs at the end of many teacher professional development events.[2]

There is no room in a school culture for teachers to lose track of students, yet it could be argued that monitoring teacher progress tends to be less systematic, without necessarily much evidence of transformation. As much as it is important for student assessment practices to evolve, so too must teacher feedback and performance reviews improve and adapt with use.

If schools are committed to improving, it makes sense that an effective feedback and assessment system for teachers should parallel the emphasis afforded to student feedback and assessment. There are many experts who weigh in on the importance of teacher feedback and reviews. This work was informed by many expert ideas including the notion that curriculum and assessment should not be separate entities, as noted by Wiggins and McTigue's (2005) view of "backward design."[3]

This initial inquiry into student assessment led to an examination of teacher assessment, which added many comprehensive and enlightened works shared by Black and Wiliam, Costa and Kallick, Danielson, Darling-Hammond, Stiggins, and more recently Reeves, Lawrence, Wormeli, and a host of educators eager to share their insights about teaching and learning experiences on LinkedIn and Facebook's Standards Based Learning and Grading group. At the core of building an expert teaching team is a process that provides specific feedback, recognition for exceptional practice, and recommendations for further growth.

Developing a performance review framework process requires concerted attention to clear criteria; such expectations should align with peer-reviewed educational research. Vazquez's (2020) dissertation addressed the impact of Costa and Kallick's *Habits of Mind* as "a framework of dispositions which established a common language for teacher-participants and student-participants to use."[4] Viewing feedback and performance appraisal tools through the lens of such dispositions can aid in further improving frameworks for formal and informal use.

Feedback and performance appraisal processes for teachers should also be linked to education experiences in teacher preparation programs that provide initial certification as well as induction programs at schools or within school districts. The OECD (2013) noted that: "Assessment capacity should be reflected in teacher standards . . . in a coherent way across teacher preparation programmes."[5] An examination of teacher dispositions can influence how teachers can approach their own assessment, as well as the assessment of their students.

According to Altan, Lane, and Dottin (2017): "By associating intelligent behaviors with educational theories, we have offered a framework that teacher educators can use in teacher education programs to help develop preservice teachers' dispositions as Habits of Mind." They claim that "this framework will help teacher education programs move forward in understanding and applying dispositions in teacher education: it offers clearly defined intelligent behaviors that can be developed using research from well-grounded educational theories."[6]

Continued work on establishing essential qualities of teachers is an important priority in schools, given the significant impact teachers have on student learning. There can be many dimensions of teacher feedback and performance reviews that schools and school systems could use as documentation for part of a teacher's formal evaluation. Marshall (2014) developed six domains for addressing teacher performance. His rubrics require supervisors "to make frequent, short, unannounced classroom visits (at least ten per teacher per year)" and "have a face-to-face coaching conversation after each one."[7]

Marshall's process involves teachers meeting formally three times a year with their supervisor in addition to self-assessing their work in relation to two or three improvement goals. When the teacher and supervisor meet they "discuss any differences, assess progress on the teacher's goals, and identify areas for growth." Finally, at the end of the school year, the teacher and supervisor "repeat this process and reach closure on the year's ratings (the supervisor, of course, has the final say).[8]

Given the importance of quality teaching in schools, there is a need for teachers and supervisors to address teaching not simply on what is observed, but what is observed relative to research-based effective practices and, ideally, collegially-set goals. Danielson's (2013) Framework for Teaching[9] was a popular tool for providing feedback and reviewing professional teaching competence. Her framework coordinates 76 teaching competencies within four domains: Planning and Preparation, the Classroom Environment, Instruction, and Professional Responsibilities.

Each competency represents a depth and breadth of educational research. Such a detailed tool can provide deliberate and specific formative feedback, at the same time as making explicit research-informed practices. While Danielson's framework could be used to provide deliberate and specific formative feedback, it was often reformed and used in a point-scoring fashion, in some cases spitting out teacher ratings as percentages.

Darling-Hammond's SoLD model[10] outlines principles of practice that feature four key interrelated components for examining the science of learning and development based on the needs of students in a classroom, namely a Supportive Environment, Productive Instructional Strategies, Social and Emotional Development and Systems of Support.

The exact wording of expectations on Marshall, Costa, and Kallick's and Danielson's tools can vary, but their intent is aimed at applying research of informed practice to support and guide ongoing teacher development. By making explicit current research, including Darling-Hammond's SoLD Principles of Practice and Dweck's Growth Mindset[11], it is possible for schools and school systems to examine their existing feedback and performance appraisal tools through new lenses that can contribute to more widespread positive teacher transformation.

An Emergent Teacher Feedback Lens emerged through use in charter and independent schools. It includes two preparation lenses: professionalism and planning; and two action lenses: culture of respect and instruction and assessment. The Emergent Teacher Feedback Lens model (Figure 8.1) provides an alternative teacher feedback and/or evaluation tool, noting that criteria should remain flexible enough to include new practices that merge new research on informed practices for ideal teaching and learning conditions.

In this adapted model, teacher assessment can be viewed as part of a feedback cycle beginning and ending with professional development in mind.

Ideally, teachers would self-assess to set specific goals with their mentors or supervisors to coordinate targeted professional development. Examples of criteria (see Tables 8.1 though 8.4) organized within four lenses can be used for self-assessment, and supervisor feedback, as well. In this model, 129 criteria are spread out throughout the lenses with evidence assessed as A, P, or

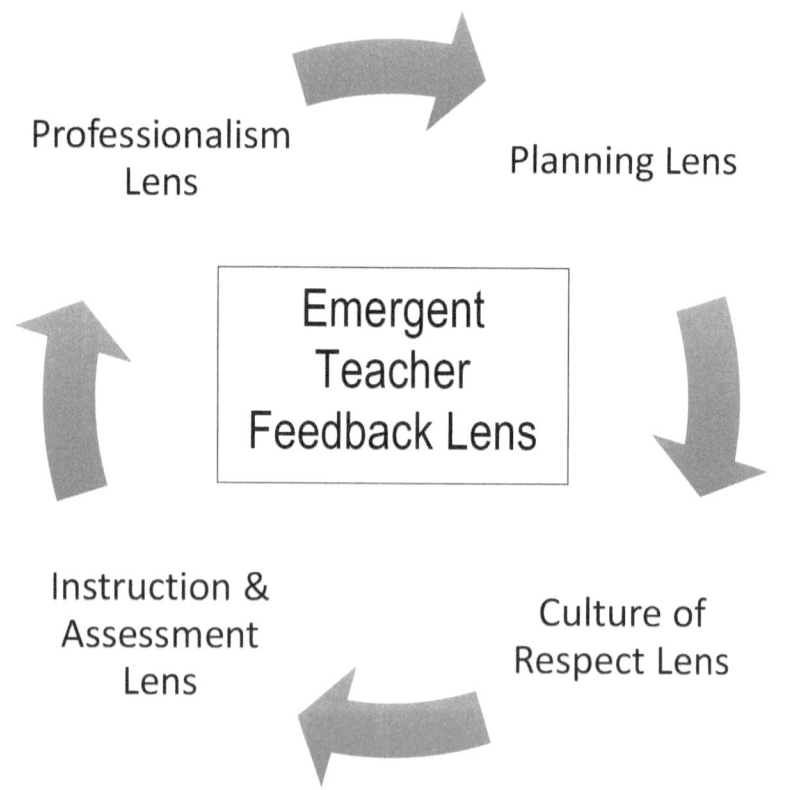

Figure 8.1. Emergent Teacher Feedback Lens Model

Table 8.1: A. Professionalism Feedback Lens

Self-Assessment	A. PROFESSIONALISM FEEDBACK LENS A= Ample evidence; P = Progressing evidence; NY = not yet provided evidence	Supervisor/Mentor Teacher Feedback
	Teacher Knowledge & Understanding. The teacher . . .	
	has teaching certification as required by government or sanctioned jurisdiction.	
	uses strategic plan to inform teaching plans to support school improvement.	
	has a strong grasp of the knowledge of the subject matter.	
	has a solid understanding of child development.	
	has an excellent level of knowledge of teaching and learning research.	
	Creative and Critical Thinker. The teacher . . .	
	is open to learning about and implementing new teaching practices.	
	engages in action research to enhance teaching and learning culture.	
	contributes valuable ideas and expertise on teacher teams and committees	
	presents at conferences to share effective innovative practices with others.	
	contributes proactive ideas and action to support school improvement.	
	Commitment. The teacher . . .	
	values the overall direction of the school (mission, vision, and strategic plan).	
	carries out school assignments conscientiously.	
	demonstrates respect through ethical and honest action.	
	collaborates with colleagues to plan units, share ideas, and analyze student work.	
	is a positive team player and contributes ideas, and time to overall school mission.	
	inspires others to support a culture of improved student learning.	
	frequently volunteers for extracurricular or cocurricular activities.	
	is punctual (respectfully begins and ends all school-related activities on time).	
	Communication. The teacher . . .	
	respects school norms and policies in words and actions.	
	listens to viewpoints and responds constructively to suggestions and criticism.	
	reflects and discusses with colleagues how to continuously improve instruction.	

> seeks feedback from students, parents, and colleagues to improve performance.
> respects confidentiality.
> responds to communications within 24 hours.
> in professional contexts, speaks and writes correctly, succinctly, and eloquently.
> keeps accurate and meticulous records.
> dresses in professional attire

Comments: (documented in email or document attached to email after a discussion of at least two areas of strengths and three areas for improvement).

NY designations: (A) refers to "ample" evidence; (P) refers to some evidence as "progress"; and (NY) indicates that the teacher or the supervisor or mentor does "not yet" see the evidence of identified specific practices.

Just as there are too many options for grading students (i.e., A, B, C, D, and F) can make the results less reliable for other teachers to duplicate, so too can too many options for assessing teachers be difficult for different school administrators to replicate. Fewer qualifier options (A, P, and NY) were designated to reduce subjectivity and increase trust in the feedback tool. When results vary from user to user, the fairness of the instrument can come into question.

An effective performance review should involve many steps that include self-assessment, school leader/supervisor/mentor assessment, as well as an examination of a teacher's professional portfolio with presentation opportunities. Teachers should have a chance to elaborate on their contributions to a school.

Often rubrics will combine different expectations under one cell, which can be confusing when the user of the tool agrees that parts of the description are present, while other parts are not. Rather than combine criteria in a given cell, the Teacher Feedback Lens attempts to keep the feedback for each cell specific to one expectation. Whether for students or teachers, it is valuable to demonstrate the difference between quality and weak work.

Teacher feedback or appraisal tools that address the descriptions of weak teacher practice do not appear helpful. For instance, one tool includes "Meets infrequently with colleagues, and conversations lack educational substance." The absence of an ideal expectation should be clear enough.

Rather than describe four scenarios, which increases the volume of the read, a clear description of expectations should suffice. One ideal crafted once has promising potential for focusing attention on the goal, rather than four derivatives of it. Where a teacher has provided some evidence of "progressing" toward an effective practice, or has "not yet" provided evidence, they can work with the supervisor, who can help set targets, in addition to coordinating supports that can lead to positive transformation and growth.

The popular use of four levels in many mainstream appraisal tools can be highly subjective. What requires improvement also does not meet standards. To some supervisors, a teacher's work may be viewed as highly effective, but to others, only effective.

For a tool to be trusted, the use should produce feedback that is replicable. Similarly, the letter grade system has much value in clarifying excellent work (A), work that is progressing toward mastery (B), but the rest of the distinctions (C, D, or F) seem to be engineering depths of weakness, when anything less than a B should not be meeting standards, and therefore require different supports and student action to achieve a B level of proficiency.

Rather than view each Teacher Feedback Lens as a cumbersome series of checklists, attending to two goals at a time, from one lens at a time, enables the feedback process to be a connected and continual long-term growth experience. The supervisor or mentor can then work with the teacher to coordinate customized professional development and support so the teacher can build more evidence to reach at least a "progressing" level of achievement (i.e., two pieces of evidence) or "ample" evidence, which would be three or more examples or instances demonstrated.

Tables 8.1 and 8.2 represent sample feedback lens forms that focus on professionalism and planning. The examples in Tables 8.3 and 8.4 require classroom observation and meeting time to reflect on the links between the planning and professional side of being a teacher and what actually happens in the context of the classroom, namely culture building and instruction and assessment.

What's Not Part of the Teacher Feedback Lens

It was surprising that some criteria used for performance reviews included "solid attendance." It seems redundant if other criteria indicate that teachers need to effectively carry out their school assignments. It would be impossible for professional educators to meet the expectations listed in many of the varied feedback tools without being present for their students and colleagues. While attendance may seem like an simple quantifiable metric, it does not align with the research on the effectiveness of teaching.

By including such criteria, it contributes to the idea that the teaching role is that of technician, one who punches in and out on a time clock, not recognizing the professionalism of many who spend countless hours preparing for teaching outside school hours.

Table 8.2: Planning Feedback Lens

Self-Assessment	B. PLANNING FEEDBACK LENS A= Ample evidence; P = Progressing evidence; NY = Not Yet provided evidence	Supervisor/Mentor Teacher Feedback
The Year Plans . . .		
	are aligned with high standards.	
	are linked to and contribute to scope and sequence of a progressive curriculum.	
	include resources that support the curriculum and preparation for standardized tests.	
The Unit/Project Based Plans . . .		
	complement the year plan and the overall school strategic plan.	
	emphasize the development of critical and creative thinking skills.	
	use a systematic approach to inquiry.	
	emphasize the application of knowledge and skills.	
	provide differentiated learning experiences to address and adapt to varied student learning needs, styles, and interests.	
	are authentic and relative to real-life experiences.	
	use effective mix of high-quality, multicultural learning materials.	
	are flexible enough to address world events in real time.	
	include purposeful use of media and technology.	
	use textbooks or other digital/print materials as resources.	
Assessment Plans		
	Classroom assessment is designed to access what students know.	
	Diagnostic assessment is used at the beginning of each unit/project.	
	Classroom assessment gathers evidence of material directly taught within unit/project.	
	Plans include different kinds of assessment that support varied learning styles.	
	Classroom assessments mirror results from standardized tests if such tests are used.	
	Classroom assessment supports student learning.	
	Plans include time set aside for collaboration with colleagues about student work and assessment data to fine-tune teaching, re-teach, and help struggling students.	
The Lesson Plans . . .		

	are aligned and support the goals/outcomes of the standards-based unit/project plan.
	break down complex tasks.
	address misconceptions and potentially confusing aspects of subject matter.
	adapt to differentiated student learning needs, styles, and interests.
	are customized to support the local and school culture.
	reveal teacher's creativity through the design of innovation learning materials.
Room Plans	
	The classroom organization and arrangement of materials and displays support an inviting climate to maximize student learning.

Comments: (documented in email or document attached to email after a discussion of at least two areas of strengths and two areas for improvement).

Noticeably absent from this discussion of teacher feedback is the mention of student test scores. Using such data might make sense when it can provide some evidence of student learning. There is no evidence that points to the notion that including test scores improves teacher performance. Rather, the inclusion of such metrics simply serves to de-motivate teachers, and to shift their practice away from implementing quality teaching and learning standards. The reliance on student test scores, as key measures of teacher performance, should be challenged when systems use such outdated and unproven approaches.

Furthermore, every school population includes a critical mass of students with varied intellectual capacity, and, thus, it would be unfair to make student scores a factor in a staff performance review. The fact is that all schools are not populated with the same kids, with the same home experiences, eating the same breakfasts, riding in the same car, using the same dental health plan, buying things with the same family income, or having the same distribution of students with special needs. Not addressing such variables makes any comparative measure of student test scores simply unfair.

It's stunning when some districts, particularly in the United States, use upwards of 50% of a percentage score as heavily weighted portions of a teacher's performance review. Such practices erode trust and quality teaching. People who support such practices have simply not read the research from education assessment experts.

The Teacher Feedback Lens differs from other assessment tools in that it does not pool together the findings for a holistic evaluation of a specific

Table 8.3: Culture of Respect Lens

		Supervisor/Designated
Self	**C. CULTURE OF RESPECT LENS**	Mentor
	A= Ample evidence; P = Progressing evidence; NY = Not Yet provided evidence	

Respectful Classroom Culture.

- The classroom is a healthy and safe environment.
- The students have a positive relationship with their teacher.
- The teacher conveys enjoyment and enthusiasm.
- The students express happiness to be on-task.
- The teacher treats students fairly.
- The teacher uses motivating incentives and rewards in a fair manner.
- The students demonstrate fairness with each other and the sharing of materials.
- Diversity is accepted (racial, ethnic, religious, gender, disabilities, and cultural differences).
- The teacher creates a trusting culture that supports creativity, discovery, and risk-taking.
- The students are supported to learn from their mistakes.
- The teacher uses classroom management techniques that ensure positive student behavior.
- The teacher and students co-construct and act on classroom rules and norms.
- Students demonstrate self-disciplined learning habits.
- Students take responsibility for their own learning and set challenging but achievable goals.
- The teacher uses cooperative learning strategies, where students support one another.
- The teacher uses real-life examples to address the importance of collegiality in the workforce.
- The teacher clarifies high expectations for classroom work and behavior.
- Students demonstrate pride in their work.
- Students demonstrate a strong sense of efficacy and confidence.
- Students organize and lead activities (class discussions, plays . . .).
- The teacher reinforces student behavior with positive support.
- Students take responsibility for their actions.
- Students use class time to maximize learning.

Teacher's Respectful Relationships with Families.

The teacher welcomes family members as key partners in the education of their children.
The teacher contacts and works with all parents, including those who may be hard to reach.
The teacher demonstrates respect for family and community culture, values, and beliefs.
The teacher updates parents on student strengths, as well as immediately flagging concerns.
The teacher addresses and responds respectfully to parent concerns.
The teacher sets up semester conferences with students and parents together to recognize student strengths and provide helping suggestions for ongoing growth and improvement.
The teacher shares with parents work examples that relate to exemplars about learning.
The teacher communicates with user-friendly language.
The teacher gives parents access to exemplar samples of student work.

Comments: (documented in email or document attached to email after a discussion of at least two areas of strengths and three areas for improvement).

Table 8.4: Instruction & Assessment Lens

Self	D. INSTRUCTION & ASSESSMENT LENS A= Ample evidence; P = Progressing evidence; NY = Not Yet provided evidence	Supervisor/ Designated Mentor
	Students take diagnostic assessments to determine what is known in advance of unit.	
	The teacher explains value of learning tasks and uses inspiring "hooks" for engagement.	
	The teacher and students can articulate the goals for learning.	
	The teacher chunks material for differentiating and scaffolding activities.	
	The teacher adapts lesson to address misunderstandings.	
	The teacher gives students wait time or "soak time" to master understanding.	
	The teacher presents activities within lessons and units in a logical manner.	
	The teacher applies the subject matter to real-life situations.	
	The teacher involves all students in problem-solving activities.	
	Students are productively engaged in activities; they lose themselves in their work.	
	Teacher develops multiple literacies (i.e., reading, writing, numeracy, scientific inquiry).	
	Students apply expert vocabulary to enhance mastery.	
	The teacher highlights the difference between mastery and weak work.	
	The teacher provides meaningful immediate feedback during lessons and for assignments.	
	Students transition between activities with little loss of instructional time.	
	The teacher uses formative feedback to adjust ongoing lessons within a unit.	
	Student work highlighting strengths is posted and celebrated.	
	Students set ambitious goals, and self-assess how well they are achieving them.	
	Students edit and revise their original work.	
	The teacher uses many learning styles and strategies to support individual student needs.	
	The teacher uses and finds engaging instructional materials and technology.	
	The teacher uses authentic audiences to enhance purpose of students' work.	
	The teacher provides experiences that lead to valuable habit formation.	
	The teacher provides students with reflective opportunities (metacognitive strategies).	
	The teacher engages students in comparing and making distinctions.	

> The teacher uses paired and group instruction for dialogue and decision-making.
> The teacher expects students to demonstrate critical and creative thinking.
> The teacher uses reciprocal teaching methods to reinforce understanding.
> The teacher celebrates student work/actions that demonstrate initiative.
> The teacher follows up with struggling students providing personal attention.
> The teacher ensures that students in need receive appropriate services immediately.
> The teacher ensures mastery of summarizing evidence and record keeping.
> The teacher enlists volunteers and community members to enrich curriculum.
> The teacher gives additional opportunities to upgrade work to learn from mistakes.
> The teacher uses tools that require students to self-assess their work and work habits.
> The teacher provides students with opportunities to build learning portfolios.
> The teacher gives students opportunities to improve the lesson or material.

Comments: (documented in email or document attached to email after a discussion of at least two areas of strengths and two areas for improvement).

domain or overall performance. There are no numbers that tempt the makings of a percentage grade or scored grouping. Summative ratings, or averaging of each expectation, are not the same as gathering professional feedback.

The purpose of the feedback lens is to make clear what is currently accepted by experts as quality practice, and to give teachers, mentors, and supervisors a specific context for supporting ongoing improvement. The Teacher Feedback Lens, like a carefully constructed survey, can serve as a tool to communicate currently informed practices.

Professional Portfolios

Teachers can use the feedback lens for self-assessment purposes; likewise, supervisors can also use such evidence of growth, or not, for both feedback and performance review. Viewing the history of increased evidence of informed practice over time within a professional portfolio can yield valuable trends in performance. At the end of the school year, it would be important for each teacher and the school leader or designated supervisor to reflect on strengths and areas for improvements. The portfolio can help capture the depth and breadth of professional evidence.

According to Croft, Cogshall, Dolan, Powers, and Killion (2010), portfolios can shine a light on a teacher's body of work. They can "track a teacher's development in a competency area" by examining and acknowledging lesson plans, reflective writing, student work, and "other materials that are used to prepare for teaching or are used directly in the classroom." This body of work can be a reference for other teachers, as well. Job-Embedded Professional Development (JEPD) can be a powerful upshot when teachers present their portfolios "to a group of one's peers" or coach.[12]

Teacher feedback over time can provide evidence of teacher transformation, which should be reflected in a professional portfolio. On an annual basis teachers can update their portfolios to include their reflections on their practice, new initiatives, and the feedback gleaned from key areas such as professionalism, planning, classroom culture, and instruction and assessment. Such a professional meeting where the portfolio is shared with a supervisor should last at least an hour in length, as the supervisor will need time to examine such a document extensively.

The portfolio should address the goals set, if they were met, and what surprises emerged throughout the school year. An ideal portfolio would contain samples of student work, media samples (i.e., photographs, video footage) as well as links to online materials developed to enhance teaching and learning. Part of a supervisor's role is to make a determination about the quality of teachers in a school.

At the end of the school year, there should be an extensive body of evidence that can contribute to the determination of whether a staff member is making an exceptional, proficient, or inadequate contribution to the school. An exceptional contributor demonstrates sustained passion, energy, and support for the school and others. A proficient contributor meets required expectations; however, this teacher would need to plan for and enhance more evidence of "exceptional practices." A teacher who receives an inadequate evaluation would require additional supports to help with significant changes in practice.

Recognizing strengths is a key piece of the performance review process. Narrowing areas for improvement promotes a culture that accepts growth and the making of mistakes as part of a learning organization—one focused on making a difference in the lives of students and community members.

Professional portfolios can be a source for both reflective and future planning purposes. The following sample portfolio (Table 8.5) illustrates how formative evidence from the Teacher Feedback Lens can contribute and be

Table 8.5: Sample Portfolio Outline

NAME:		
• GRADE LEVEL/SUBJECT TAUGHT • TABLE OF CONTENTS • UPDATED RESUME • FORMAL OBSERVATION REVIEWS • EVIDENCE of PROFESSIONAL DEVELOPMENT • REFLECTIONS ON GOALS SET & MET		
SELF REVIEW	*PORTFOLIO REVIEW and ASSESSMENT CRITERIA*	*SCHOOL LEADER FEEDBACK*
	3 **EXCEPTIONAL** (portfolio provides ample evidence of student understandings, innovative curriculum design, work exceeds expectations) 3 **PROFICIENT** (portfolio meets most requirements) 3 **NOT YET** (parts of portfolio are lacking)	
	A. PROFESSIONALISM	
	B. PLANNING	
	C. CULTURE OF RESPECT	
	D. INSTRUCTION & ASSESSMENT	
	TEACHER-LEADER (Option)	
	Evidence of PROFESSIONAL DEVELOPMENT	
	Meeting Professional Goals	
	***Meets requirements of Portfolio	

OVERALL EVALUATION

Exceptional Contribution	Proficient Contribution	Inadequate Contribution

Supervisor Signature: _____
Date: _____

aligned and included as part of a composite design of a quality professional portfolio.

How supervisors make determinations of overall evaluations should require a synthesis of many sources. In addition to school leaders reflecting on the teacher portfolios, they should keep records of their rounds of mini classroom visits, communications, parent and student feedback, as well as the teacher and supervisory feedback. Using the sample feedback lenses can provide a depth and breadth of evidence. The value of informal regular mini classroom visits should not be minimized.

Just as immediate feedback is key to supporting student learning, the practice of supervisors gathering evidence of teacher strengths, or possible areas for improvement, should be relayed in a timely manner. The informal gathering of evidence in these scenarios enables school leaders to contribute to what teachers share in their portfolios, in addition to expanding the evidence for making evaluative decisions about overall performance.

Implementing a Robust Feedback and Performance Review Process

The purpose of implementing a robust performance review process should be to support the building of a critical mass of "exceptional teachers" within a school. Carefully designed feedback systems can involve the coordination of formal classroom observations, professional review of follow-up teaching meetings, and follow-through e-mail communications and portfolio reflections.

Formal Classroom Observations for Teaching Staff

Formal classroom observations should happen at least twice a year for at least a full lesson, ideally for sixty or more minutes at a time. It's important for a supervisor to experience a class from start to finish, as the students do. A drop-in assessment for 10 to 15 minutes is not enough time to experience the full context of a lesson, and what students experience. Additional observations might be added for new teachers to the profession, or teachers who may require additional support. Observations can also include data collected from regular rounds.

During the observation, the supervisor can use the same form that teachers originally used to self-evaluate their teaching strengths. During the formal observation, the supervisor can determine whether the practices are evident, or not, and focus additional attention on the goals designated by the teacher, and the supervisor. The reviewer keeps a running record of as much evidence as possible gathered about observed lessons. As well, the school principal, or designate, should document weekly rounds of crosswalks in every classroom to discuss any similarities or variances from the formal observation settings.

Follow-Up Observation Meetings

The principal or designate should set up a meeting immediately following an observation. It should last at least 30 minutes, with a limit of approximately one hour. All participants should be able to request additional time to clear up any questions.

In the first meeting, the supervisor should ask questions about the context of the class (i.e., what lessons happened prior; where the lesson is headed in the future), while sharing strengths and offering recommendations for future consideration. Ideally, this conversation happens the same day or the next day. An initial observation would provide evidence to clarify whether goals are being met, and whether additional goals should be set. The second observation meeting would focus on changes in practice and how well goals are met, and whether the teacher has applied improved practices in other classroom situations.

Follow- through E-mail/Written Documentation

After the Follow-up Observation Meeting, the supervisor should forward the assessment with a personal message via e-mail or in paper form. Teachers should be encouraged to house this copy of the document in their professional portfolio binder. The following letter to Ms. P features a sample follow-through e-mail after an observation of a grade 3 math class:

Dear Ms. P,

Thank you for the opportunity to view your math class yesterday . . . First, I'm thrilled our grade 3 math students have Ms. P . . . I am convinced students who have this kind of math class everyday are experiencing what has the potential to be a Tier 1 experience. It is clear to me that you care deeply about being the best at your craft and this is a paramount professional quality! Your topic "what is change?" was authentic and interesting for your students. It was evident some students enjoyed sharing what they know . . . Some of the students appeared disinterested at first but the task of being a "customer" and the "piggly wiggly" cashier quickly drew all students into the mix. The students were very engaged in their partner work, negotiating the meaning and handling the subtraction of decimals . . . with ease. You were intuitive to see that the partners needed to sit on the same side of the table . . . Having the "hands-on'"bags of money available for the students to use was beneficial . . . It was evident they used "manipulatives" often.

Your voice was warm and projected well in the class. You recognized good teamwork and supported good behavior often. When the students were leading the discussion about their problem, they said "yell it out" and you kindly corrected, with "I prefer you respond in a calm way." Students responded well to your positive reinforcement, and when students needed re-directing, it might be good to try to use body language or signals that are more private messages . . . The saying "praise in public; criticize in private" can go a long way to building strong relationships with all students in your class . . . The engagement in your class was powerful. When a few students were less "productive" you spent time with them and did not let them opt out. In this case, I thought about differentiation as a possible preventative solution for the future. If the pair of students had been given two problems at a time, and then asked to show you their work, you could have rewarded them with two more problems . . .

The role-playing was wonderful, especially when the students had a chance to wear the "piggly wiggly" cashier nametag. They took the roles further when some students had a chance to go to the whiteboard and do the question by asking each other: "Customer, what did you pay?" This truly brought the question to life. Having students lead the way at the board is always a great sign of quality teaching . . .

Moving to them, not them moving to you is the stuff of great teaching . . . What I would add to your tool kit would be a class list—so that you could track each pairing, and document something about their level of understanding of "change" as you went along. Daily documented assessment is something we will focus on in professional development for all the staff. Exit tickets give you a chance to review what students need the next day when they return to continue to explore the relationship between change and operations.

When we met to discuss your class, I was also impressed with your eagerness to gain insight into your classroom. You were open to suggestions and presented a professional manner that makes me proud to say you are on staff. I'm thrilled that you are part of our team . . .

Respectfully, Barbara Smith, Principal

The purpose of such personal messages is to add to the credibility of the process. Teachers appreciate such customizing of the observation, at the same time as a clear direction based on the informed practices embedded within each of the four lenses. The tools, the personal response, and the conversations also serve to kick-start further professional development, as the supervisor can explain why the criteria matters in the context of the school.

Reference Letters and Summative Feedback

At the end of the school year, school leaders, or designates, can write each teacher a reference letter taking into account the strengths documented from a variety of evidence sources. Seasoned administrators can model the process of reference letter writing, so future school leaders could learn and emulate how to pen professional and personal communications. Such work can take an incredible amount of time, depending on the number of letters written, but such efforts can be well worth the investment.

Weaving Professional Development, Feedback, and Performance Review

Prior to the beginning of the school year, teachers should be asked to complete a self-assessment of each lens as a prediction of how they plan and implement informed teaching practices. A 30- to 45-minute discussion of the items with a supervisor would help secure at least two goals from each lens for targeting feedback. This information can help supervisors provide specific supports throughout the school year. At the end of the school year, the supervisor will discuss not only the evidence gathered throughout the year (in the teacher's portfolio), but also how well the teacher goals were met.

Ideally, formal reviews of classroom observations happen twice a year so teachers have an opportunity to show improvement in the same academic year with the same group of students in a similar teaching context. It makes sense for new staff members to be reviewed near the end of a shorter introductory period (i.e., 30 days) in addition to their two formal reviews.

As part of teacher-leadership initiatives, seasoned mentor teachers can be enlisted to take part in the feedback process. The documentation from all feedback sources can guide professional development. Teachers can benefit from summative formal documentation, in addition to a healthy serving of formative and informal feedback throughout the overall review process.

Team Planning and Teaching as Ongoing Development and Observation

The more feedback teachers can receive with direct reference to the context of their classrooms, the better the opportunity for growth and improvement. Schools that are organized with a ratio of eight or less direct reports for one supervisor can manage a thorough and comprehensive feedback system. Quality control over any institution is limited when a supervisor is responsible for too many direct reports at the same time. Many teachers engage in professional learning communities, some facilitated by coaches or supervisors, some not.

One school in DC introduced further steps in coaching that involved the practice of co-planning and teaching, which enabled exceptional teachers (supervisors/mentors/coaches) to provide ongoing support to less seasoned teachers or those in need of improvement. Some coaches often shared ideas through demonstration lessons, which can be valuable for teachers to be observers of informed practice.

Rather than relying on a few demonstrations and professional conversations, schools might consider expanding the coaching role to include regular co-planning followed by co-teaching so that supervisors and mentors can gain a deeper understanding of the classroom context and, therefore, be more able to provide rich feedback for teachers, both informally, and formally. By including co-planning and co-teaching in the professional growth and review cycle, it is possible for teachers to have more frequent informal classroom visits, with at least two formal observations and follow-ups per year.

For comprehensive performance reviews to take place, it can be ideal for schools to consider new structures that encourage more exceptional teachers to become teacher-leaders. A flattening of the traditional organizational chart can permit more exceptional teachers to be in their own classrooms for part of the day, giving students direct access to informed teaching, while the other half of the day, such coaches can work with teachers in need of ongoing supports via co-planning and teaching.

Building in regular time for mentors to teach with the teacher in the context of the classroom at the same time can contribute significantly to gathering evidence of ongoing improvement. Discussions between coaches and teachers about the criteria in each teacher feedback lens in the context of a shared classroom teaching experience can contribute both to the development of the teacher, as well as the teacher-leader. On many occasions the mentor teachers bring new resources to the table to work collegially with teachers, to provide ongoing customized professional development.

Sample Timeline for PD and Teacher Feedback

Feedback frameworks should address precision; however, defining the timing of meetings and professional development activities should permit customization so such detailing can align with the school structure. For instance, how often teachers meet can depend on whether schools have ample PD Days built into each term. Teachers should meet to collegially design units, but when weekly hour slots are mandated, it is not enough time to co-design a quality unit. Ideally, teachers would have full or half days carved out on a schedule, so clarifying the timing would be dependent on a host of factors.

It is important that feedback tools set criteria that would not minimize the commitment, and allow for schools to define what time is needed for ongoing curriculum construction, check-ins, and reflections on student experiences.

Based on the assumption that a school could be divided into three terms, using three traditional break times in North American schools: winter break (end of December), spring break (begins near the end of March), and summer break (begins at the end of June). A coordinated timing cycle for feedback in the context of professional development can involve ongoing professional growth that could include summer PD, term PD, monthly PD, weekly PD, formal observations, and a time after school ends for portfolio review with final appraisal.

Summer PD:

- Teachers self-assess each of four Teacher Feedback Lenses.
- Teachers use Professionalism and Planning Feedback lenses to set goals with their supervisor based on discussion of professional materials and plans.
- Teachers engage in a "Backward Design" Workshop to link curriculum with assessment.

Term PD (3 full days):

- Day 1 (i.e., October)—discussion of Cultures of Respect lens; teachers set two goals focused on enhancing a culture of respect within the classroom, school, and community members
- Day 2 (i.e., December)—focus on report card entries; focus on instruction and assessment expectations
- Day 3 (i.e., March)—teachers work on portfolios and report card entries

Monthly PD:

- Monthly curriculum meetings (to design and reflect on the teaching and learning of the unit)
*2-hour early dismissal

Weekly PD:

- Weekly team planning and team teaching (supervisor/designate and teacher)
- Teachers reflecting on two goals identified from Professionalism and Planning lenses

Formal Observation, Meeting, Follow-up E-mail:

- First formal teacher observation and focus on Instruction & Assessment Feedback lens (1)
- Teachers set two instruction and assessment goals after follow-up meeting about classroom observation (1)
- Second formal teacher observation and discussion of Instruction and Assessment Feedback lens, as well as movement toward achieving goals set in December (2)

End of Year Appraisal:

- Portfolio discussion and performance evaluation

Building in early dismissals can permit at least a two-hour time slot for collaboration, which gives teachers more ongoing opportunities to work collegially.

A Deep Record of Professional Development

A portfolio may include samples of readings and practices as documented in professional books and articles. Teachers should also be abreast of progressive ideas outside the school or district. Attending workshops and conferences with other professionals can help teachers build more extensive networks as well as explore alternative perspectives on teaching and learning practices.

In Canada, leveled coaching courses have been developed for a wide variety of sports. Parents who volunteer as soccer or hockey coaches in their little leagues, for instance, were required to be certified by a nationally accredited set of coaching standards. Many physical education teachers add such coaching credentials to their resumes. The Red Cross and other safety agencies also offer CPR and first aid micro-credentials for teachers, usually prior to the beginning of school. As much as micro-credentials can be significant for student learning, they can be value-added components to augment performance reviews.

Portfolio assessment should include professional development experiences, which can include micro-credentialing in a vast number of areas related to education. Katrina Schwartz from *MindShift* (2017) interviewed, Kettle Moraine's superintendent, Patricia Deklotz, about their compensation structure for teachers "so they could add to their base pay for completing micro-credentials of their choosing."[13]

Deklotz claimed that this approach "would give her teachers the chance to personalize their own professional learning, and give them some of the choice and agency that she hoped they would turn around and apply in their classrooms."[14] To receive their micro-credentials, teachers were expected to submit artifacts for review and, "if the reviewers feel the educator did not submit strong enough evidence of learning, they can provide feedback and ask the educators to try again."[15]

Supervisors that determine an overall evaluation to be less than proficient would expect to support these teachers in further efforts to provide more evidence that meets such proficiency. Dedicated funding for teacher development is worth a serious investment of funds in any school budget. It is a myth to assume that teachers, seasoned or not, would be exceptional.

The new reality that fewer young people are interested in becoming teachers makes it even more imperative to realize that supports and feedback not be limited to the short time frame in teacher preparation programs. The notion of induction and ongoing professional learning needs to be a priority for school systems; human capital needs to be developed and sustained simultaneously.

Concerned about teachers leaving the profession, Garcia and Weiss (2019) recommended that schools "tackle the working conditions and other factors that are promoting teachers to quit and dissuading people from entering the profession, thus making it harder for school districts to retain and attract highly qualified teachers: low pay, a challenging school environment, and weak professional development support and recognition." They added: "In addition to tackling these factors for all schools, we must provide extra supports and funding."[16]

The path to a critical mass of exceptional teachers cannot be through a revolving door. Although there may be cases whereby certain teachers do not have the capacity to work in every school, a powerful culture of professional and deliberate staff development can move a school forward. However, even when there may be ideal conditions in place, some teachers may require performance improvement plans to ensure they pay serious attention to their responsibilities.

Performance Improvement Plans

A focus on four feedback lenses can document how some teachers, fixed in their position of not needing to improve, may not provide evidence of growth in terms of moving from having less evidence (some or none) to ample examples of expected expectations. The Teacher Feedback Lenses can provide clear expectations and feedback, so it is up to poor performers, with the support of their supervisors/coaches, to revise their practice by providing more evidence of meeting performance expectations. As much as we expect students to improve, educators need to demonstrate growth, too.

At any given time in the school year, the school leader, perhaps in coordination with other administrators, may develop a Performance Improvement Plan (PIP) for a staff member who needs to improve their performance immediately. The staff member recommended for a PIP should have input, but ultimately the documentation and monitoring of the actions expected to demonstrate success of the plan would be the responsibility of the designated school leader.

The establishment of a comprehensive process for feedback and performance review requires a team of teacher-leaders or mentors capable of implementing a rigorous plan. Rather than investing in full-time coaches, and taking such human capital strengths out of the classrooms, it can make sense for schools to consider increasing the number of part-time leadership positions, so that teaching talent does not have to be out of reach of the students. In the next chapter the focus turns to feedback for school leaders.

All community members play a significant role in the further development of a school.

Action Items

Ask school administrators if they pause, start or study, the following:

- *Pause* the disconnect between teacher feedback, performance reviews, goal setting, and professional growth plans.
- *Pause* expecting teachers to implement too many initiatives at the same time.
- *Pause* the use of general headings on feedback tools and performance reviews.
- *Pause* using student test scores as criteria for teacher performance reviews.
- *Pause/reduce* the number of subjective qualifiers (adequate, satisfactory, good, very good, excellent, outstanding, exceptional) to give a clearer picture for improvement.
- *Pause* saying there is no room or time in the curriculum for experiential learning.
- *Start* supporting the use of professional portfolios.
- *Start* promoting teacher involvement in professional associations.
- *Start* finding funds for teachers to go to conferences.
- *Start* including more self-assessment and reflective practices as part of feedback processes and performance reviews.
- *Start* accepting practical experiences and qualifications as evidence of learning.
- *Study* survey data to gain insight into stakeholder perceptions of school experience.
- *Study* current research on quality performance reviews in schools and institutions/businesses outside the field of education.

What do you think schools need to pause, start, or study with reference to teacher feedback?

NOTES

1. Wiliam, D., & Leahy, S. (2014), p. 8, https://www.dylanwiliamcenter.com/wp-content/uploads/sites/3/2020/10/DW02-01-Chapter-X-TLC-Paper-03-05-17-Digital.pdf.

2. Ibid., 14.

3. Wiggins & McTigue (2005).
4. Costa, A., & Kallick, B. (2000), 220.
5. OECD (2013), p. 223.
6. Altan, S., Lane, J.F., & Dottin, E. (2017), 12.
7. Marshall, K. (January 2, 2014), https://www.marshallmemo.com/articles/Teacher%20rubrics%20Jan%202014%20corr.pdf.
8. Ibid.
9. Danielson, C. (2013).
10. Darling-Hammond, L. (February 17, 2019), https://www.tandfonline.com/doi/full/10.1080/10888691.2018.1537791.
11. Dweck, C., https://www.youtube.com/watch?v=hiiEeMN7vbQ.
12. Croft, A., Coggshall, J.G., Dolan, M., Powers, E., & Killion, J. (2010), 7.
13. Schwartz, K. (February 15, 2017), https://www.kqed.org/mindshift/47476/can-micro-credentials-create-meaningful-professional-development-for-teachers.
14. Ibid.
15. Ibid.
16. Garcia, E., & Weiss, E. (April 16, 2019), https://www.epi.org/publication/u-s-schools-struggle-to-hire-and-retain-teachers-the-second-report-in-the-perfect-storm-in-the-teacher-labor-market-series/.

9

Growth of School Leaders and Teacher-Leaders

What If . . .

WHAT IF SCHOOL LEADERS AND TEACHER-LEADERS RECEIVED RIGOROUS FEEDBACK COMPARABLE TO WHAT STUDENTS AND TEACHERS TAKE PART IN?

While it makes sense for schools to have a rigorous teacher feedback and performance review process, it is also important for every school employee to take part in a vigorous system that addresses feedback, performance review, and professional growth.

Feedback and Performance of the School Leadership Team

According to The Wing Institute: "The field of principal evaluation, while gaining increased research interest in recent years, lags behind teacher evaluation in terms of conclusions that can be made regarding effective practice."[1] Experts can vary on what constitutes best practice, but many would agree that a process of ongoing feedback for school leaders tends to be missing in many school systems.

Hattie (2015) noted that "the greatest influence on student progression in learning is having highly expert, inspired and passionate teachers and school leaders working together to maximise the effect of their teaching on all students in their care."[2] Focusing on the role of the school leader and school systems, he added that the system should "provide the support, time and resources" to "harness the expertise in their schools."[3]

Who provides oversight and support over a school's leadership team depends on whether a school is part of a district or whether a school has its own independent board. In the case of private schools, where the owner can be the principal, there may not be any process for systematically providing leadership feedback, performance review, or professional development.

In most public schools, it is the superintendent who provides feedback and support to the principal, and it is the principal who is responsible for providing feedback and appraising the members of his or her administrative team. In independent or charter schools, a Board of Directors would ideally have at least one or more members with a significant background in education. Such a member would be aware of the most current understandings of educational research and best practice; and, as such, this individual would be recognized as qualified to oversee the assessment of the school leader.

Just as teachers need to identify goals for development, a school leader needs to address areas for growth, as well. Professional conversations between the superintendent or board member with the school leader can help to narrow the focus for feedback, performance review, and professional development. A school leader should not be excused from the process, and therefore needs to model a willingness to embrace change and strive for improvement.

School leaders, who engage in portfolio work that includes a component of self-assessment, can align their development with the direct needs of the School Improvement Plan. Just as teachers can benefit from a feedback lens, so too can school leaders use such a tool for making explicit informed practices for any position in the school. Table 9.1 illustrates a Feedback Lens tool for a school leader that was designed and adapted for use in a variety of different school contexts.

How to customize such a tool depends on the job description of the school leader as well as the school strategic plan and specific expectations laid out when the school leader was hired. Some of the criteria above may be viewed as universal, while others more unique to a specific school. Ideally, the feedback lens would be in direct alignment with the job description.

Some schools and school systems have different kinds of options for assessing school leaders, while others do not have any system in place for supporting or developing their leadership teams. In cases where there were no feedback mechanisms, the contracts for school leaders were either renewed, or not. Ideally school leaders would go through the same emphasis on rigorous assessment as each staff member. In some schools, staff members can provide 360-degree feedback so school leaders can hear directly how well they are performing and what areas need improvement.

There tends to be a lack of rigorous assessment at the administrative level in many schools and school districts. Learning boards should lead

Table 9.1: Sample School Leader Feedback Lens

Self	SCHOOL LEADER Feedback Lens Expectations A= Ample evidence; P = Progressing evidence; NY = Not Yet provided evidence	Superintendent/ Board Member
	reports regularly to the Superintendent/ Board.	
	develops/updates and sustains school vision.	
	ensures safety and supervision for all students.	
	ensures school meets legislative requirements.	
	leads the coordination and implementation of the School Improvement Plan.	
	maintains ease of access for community members (open door policy).	
	establishes the school calendar with input from administrative team.	
	collaborates with other educational leaders and attends seminars/conferences.	
	liaises with experts at local, national, and global university institutions.	
	recommends/approves revisions/restructuring of job descriptions.	
	coaches, supervises, and evaluates staff through regular informal classroom visits.	
	coordinates recruitment, hiring, and retention of exceptional teachers and staff.	
	selects, leads, and manages the school leadership team.	
	works cooperatively with the administrative team to write staff evaluations.	
	team teaches and teaches innovative programs.	
	supervises and conducts performance reviews of administrative team.	
	manages, supervises, and evaluates non-instructional staff and duty assignments.	
	oversees, supports, and ensures positive student, staff, and community culture, coordination of volunteers, and positive relationships with the parent association.	
	oversees and supports implementation of effective curriculum, instruction, and implementation of student assessment system (reporting).	
	oversees and supports Special Education program to ensure effective services.	
	oversees and supports staff development.	
	oversees disciplinary process (suspensions, recommendation of expulsions).	
	nominates and recognizes committed staff for awards.	
	ensures the school's compliance with authorizers/accreditors.	
	ensures school's success in accreditation process.	
	seeks, writes, and applies for educational grants.	
	manages fiscal and human resources in the school capacity.	

provides oversight to ensure adequate school resources (including technology).
Comments: (documented in email or document attached to email after a discussion of at least two areas of strengths and three areas for improvement).

performance reviews of their school leaders as all educators, including the school leader, should be recipients of quality appraisals.

It's also important to consider what type of assessments are used to certify school leaders. In some jurisdictions, teachers and principals develop portfolios, while others make these individuals sit for examinations of a standardized test. At the Ontario Institute for Studies in Education (OISE) at the University of Toronto, candidates participated in two summers of coursework and were responsible for completing a collaborative practicum project.[4] A portfolio of experiences was built up over time, as well as rigorous internship experiences within the contexts of their own schools.

Many certifications are not transferable. The Department of Education in Virginia, for instance, did not recognize the OISE Principal qualification, but after persistent parent challenges in the media, they offered an opportunity for the principal to sit a three-hour test, which consisted of ninety multiple-choice questions followed by seven essays.[5] This version of rigor granted the principal temporary leadership status to be the school leader in the state for one school year. Two worlds; two value systems.

More informed ways than digital tests should determine whether someone has the capacity to lead. Moving others to action is difficult to predict from a percentage score; it seems that patterns of actions and impact should provide more sustainable evidence.

All staff in leadership roles should have a performance review that directly relates to their job description. Teacher mentors, for instance, take on teacher-leader roles, as do other specific administrative roles (principal, deans, vice-principals, directors). To be an effective mentor, a teacher-leader shares the responsibility for moving the staff in a proactive and industrious direction, supporting and contributing to the school's strategic plan, committed to ongoing school improvement.

Teacher-leaders also need to be able to read and respond to peer-reviewed research, at the same time as demonstrateing how to conduct action research in the context of their own schools. Globally, there are many pockets of teacher-researchers participating as key players and teachers in schools.

Supported by a Spencer Foundation Grant,[6] the Developing Inquiring Communities in Education Project (DICEP)[7] was established in the nineties to bring together teacher-researchers and university researchers to examine classroom interactions to discover ways to enhance student learning. Based on their work, Wells (1999) claimed that teachers and teacher educators can contribute to significant improvements through participation in school classrooms "to clarify our own understanding of what is involved in the construction and reconstruction of knowledge."[8]

Similarly, the Santa Barbara Classroom Discourse Group[9] provided an inspirational space for teacher-researchers to explore together how to improve teaching and learning. Addressing the importance of talking knowledge, Dixon and Green (2009) noted that the community "composed of teachers, researchers, and students" was concerned "with understanding how everyday life in classrooms is constructed by members through their interactions, verbal and other, and how these constructions influence what students have opportunities to access, accomplish, and thus, 'learn' in schools."[10]

Teacher-researcher roles have been supported by Jack Whitehead and his team, who use Living Theory as a viable way for teacher participants to make meaning through action research. The teacher's experiential understanding of learning contexts embeds them as a part of the solution. Whitehead's sustained work for close to four decades at the University of Bath in the UK emerged from his driving question: "How do I improve what I am doing?" Whitehead (2009) noted: "In developing this approach, I have emphasized the importance of the action researcher as a knowledge-creator in the process of seeking to improving practice."[11]

In her paper on learning as continuous professional development, "Mentoring in Living Educational Theory Cultures of Inquiry for Teacher Professionalism in Creating the Future," Jackie Delong shares insights into her experiences after introducing Living Educational Theory as a model for professional development in her role as a superintendent of education in Canada for 13 years.

Delong's team of inquiring teachers and administrators grew from seven to a "critical mass of teacher-researchers across the system."[12] They generated eight volumes of *Passion in Professional Practice*, a collection of classroom research. She noted: "I invited teachers to create their own-living-educational theories and to personalize their data." Through action-reflection cycles, Delong's team engaged in systematic inquiry. They aimed to improve practice and "make public" their educational influences, "using values as standards of judgment and explanatory principles" to expand their own and others' learning.[13]

Delong's impressive career was influenced by Whitehead, and, in turn, she has gone on to mentor many master's and doctoral level teacher-researcher candidates. To make room for more leaders like Delong, who inspire teacher-leaders to mentor, revise curriculum, write and review articles and books, present at conferences, take additional coursework, interview "new hires," engage in professional associations, apply for grants, and take part in action research, the current structuring of time in schools would need to change.

Teachers need additional preparation time for such growth, so schools committed to supporting teacher development through leadership roles need to address significant shifts in the schedule. Imagine a school crawling with teacher-leaders? Table 9.2 features a sample Teacher-Leader Performance Review that can also share the scope of what teacher-leaders can do in schools.

Some performance review processes are better than others. When they are cultivated in concert with professional growth plans, all staff have opportunities to improve. While some school leaders may use a "revolving door" to move weaker teachers out of the path of students, there are others who seek to provide a quality review experience that can help teachers improve their practice. It makes sense to invest in supportive programming.

Table 9.2: Sample Teacher-Leadership Performance Review

Self	*Teacher-Leadership*—How well did you . . . A= Ample evidence; P = Progressing evidence; NY = Not Yet provided evidence	School Leader
	model expectations of the school mission	
	model exceptional teaching in own classroom	
	establish and attain key program goals	
	develop, manage, supervise, and evaluate specific programs	
	ensure that specific curriculum follows the local guidelines and national association expectations	
	mentor and support new teachers	
	co-plan and co-teach regularly in mentee's classroom	
	ensure the integration of technology for learning in mentee's classes	
	ensure mentee provides differentiated instruction through content, process, and manipulatives to address all student's needs	
	order materials and stay within program budget	
	take part and make time to interview for hiring of program staff	
	take leadership development courses	
	seek leadership roles/positions	
	participate in a leadership role in professional organizations	
	apply to present at conferences	
	take part in action research as a teacher-researcher	
	write reviews of professional books	
	write professional articles/curriculum	
	seek, write, and apply for educational grants	
	ensure that mentees maintain a personal appearance that displays cleanliness, modesty, good taste, and support of school policy	
	ensure that mentees represent the school in a professional manner	

Comments: (documented in email or document attached to email after a discussion of at least two areas of strengths and three areas for improvement).

It's naïve to assume that it is easy to replace weaker teachers with exceptional educators, as if there is a steady stream of strong teachers waiting in the wings to be hired. The grass is not always greener on the other side of that revolving door. It may seem like a simple answer to let weaker employees go, to make room for stronger professionals, but there are no guarantees that new hires would automatically be better. School administrators have a responsibility to develop their teachers.

Developing professionally does not need to be void of fun. One school leader decided to reward teachers who displayed different *habits of mind* during a summer PD day session. Sixty-three staff members were awarded bananas and zucchinis with professional traits labelled by black markers and stickers to salute and reinforce the finding and celebrating of many of their strengths. The week was not about threats or fearmongering centered on a mandate of achieving high test scores. The week wound down with a simple celebration honoring a host of informed practices. Feedback can be informal and fun.

Just as ranking for students reduces the assessment process to winners and losers, it can have the same demoralizing impact for staff. For a team to succeed, it has to be the goal of school leadership to increase the critical mass of exceptional employees. It should not be a mystery how staff members in schools are evaluated. Teachers, school leaders, and teacher-leaders should be encouraged to self-assess and reflect on their experiences.

Too many performance reviews are not only rigid, but lack the depth and breadth that a quality portfolio can bring. As Mehta and Fine (2017) point out: "With lack of teacher freedom comes lack of student freedom, and disengagement and tuning out."[14] If teachers remain such a critical force in schools, school leaders need to make sure the way they are assessed respects their freedom and their capacity to be designers of better ways of teaching and learning.

Action Items

Ask school administrators if they can pause, start or study the following:

- *Pause* the disconnect between feedback, goal setting, and professional growth plans.
- *Pause* the use of general headings only for performance reviews.
- *Pause/reduce* the number of subjective qualifiers (adequate, satisfactory, good, very good, excellent, outstanding, exceptional) to give a clearer picture for improvement.
- *Start* supporting the use of professional portfolios.
- *Start* assessing school leaders and teacher-leaders.

- *Start* promoting teacher-leader involvement in professional associations.
- *Start* encouraging teachers, teacher-leaders, and school leaders to engage in action research.
- *Start* finding funds for teachers to go to and, better yet, present at conferences.
- *Study* survey data to gain insight into stakeholder perceptions of school experience.
- *Study* about leadership by reviewing websites such as https://www.creativeleadership.net; https://commongroundcollaborative.org; and https://www.actionresearch.net/.
- *Study* current research on quality performance reviews in schools and institutions/businesses outside the field of education.

What do you think schools need to pause, start, or study with reference to assessing school leaders?

NOTES

1. The Wing Institute, https://www.winginstitute.org/quality-leadership-principal-evaluation).
2. Hattie, J. (June, 2015), 2, https://www.pearson.com/content/dam/corporate/global/pearson-dot-com/files/hattie/150526_ExpertiseWEB_V1.pdf.
3. Ibid., 23.
4. Ontario Institute for Studies in Education (OISE) at the University of Toronto, https://cpl.oise.utoronto.ca/program_certificate/principals-qualification-program/.
5. https://www.washingtonpost.com/local/education/loudoun-county-charter-school-principal-denied-administrators-license/2014/12/10/966eae38-808a-11e4-8882-03cf08410beb_story.html.
6. Spencer Foundation Grant, https://www.spencer.org.
7. Developing Inquiring Communities in Education Project (DICEP), https://www.researchgate.net/publication/227193287_DICEP_Promoting_Collaborative_Inquiry_in_Diverse_Educational_Settings.
8. Wells, G. (1999), 53.
9. Dixon, C.N., & Green, J. (March, 2009), Santa Barbara Classroom Discourse Group, https://www.jstor.org/stable/41483538.
10. Ibid.
11. Whitehead, J. (2009), 95, https://journals.sagepub.com/doi/abs/10.1177/1476750308099599.
12. Delong, J. (2021), 2.

13. Ibid., 6.
14. Mehta, J., & Fine, S. (2017), https://www.gse.harvard.edu/news/ed/17/01/why-periphery-often-more-powerful-core.

10

Growth of Non-Instructional Staff
What If . . .

WHAT IF NON-INSTRUCTIONAL SCHOOL STAFF RECEIVED MORE RIGOROUS FEEDBACK?

Staff members in a school who do not take on the role of teacher can vary. They can include members of the office support staff, business managers, admission coordinators, and food services coordinators. While much attention in schools is paid to the teaching staff, it is also important to ensure rigorous feedback systems exist for non-instructional staff. Often these individuals provide incredible support for schools, yet many may not receive much formal feedback about their work. Some of the most compassionate and enthusiastic faces of a school are the security personnel and members of the maintenance teams and office staff.

It makes sense that all employees benefit from regular feedback and opportunities for professional growth. Meeting to discuss plans, checking in during project work, and making time to reflect on work completed, with reference to one's job description, enables a supervisor to take part in the goal setting and adjusting process. Waiting until the end of the year to submit a final grade takes away the opportunity to support improvement in action, to promote further positive pro-action.

The clarity of the job description can help ensure professional conversations focus on the needs of the organization. According to Murphy (2019): "Making the job description part of the performance review process is key for checking in with how well an individual's goals align with the organisation's objectives." He mentioned that aligning job descriptions with the organization's objective can help keep staff "going in one direction." Murphy added:

"Writing a good job description is a skill in itself, and many companies lack understanding about what should be included."[1]

A performance review that is aligned with non-instructional staff job descriptions can give the school leadership an opportunity to support and celebrate work behind the teaching and learning scenes. In addition to reception duties, for instance, at one school, they formalized different office staff positions so there were specific "go-to" people for technology, data coordination, food services, and admissions. Rather than referring to these individuals as general office staff, everyone had designated parts to play and, as such, served as coordinators of specific responsibilities.

By designating roles with doable multiple responsibilities, a school can also save money. At one school, the technology coordinator was also a STEM teacher. The job description listed the following hybrid responsibilities:

- establishes a positive rapport with students, parents, staff, and the public
- teaches robotics and drones, coding, podcasting, web design, yearbook design, and film production
- stays up to date on current technology supports for learning
- supports staff with technology needs (Smartboard, projectors, Google Docs)
- coordinates technology workshops to enhance staff use of technology with students
- recommends and implements school systems software
- updates the school website
- manages general email accounts for staff
- arranges for telecommunication or technology repairs
- ensures smooth operation of equipment (computers, etc.)
- supervises during designated lunch or recess duty

Table 10.1 illustrates the related feedback lens outlined for such a position.

Table 10.2 illustrates a sample Receptionist and Data Coordinator Feedback Lens.

Whether providing feedback for students, teachers, school leaders, teacher-leaders, or non-instructional staff, it is important that any tool used to guide professional conversations be flexible enough to change. New expectations based on research into best practices or a school's need to restructure may be reason to adjust expectations; however, these should not change midyear. The need to be explicit about modifying expectations should happen prior to the signing of contracts.

Keeping the dimensions of feedback to three levels of evidence (i.e., ample, some, and none) reduces the rater's potential bias. London's (2001) research addressed the assumption that "ratings measure the performance

Table 10.1: Sample Technology Manager and STEM Teacher Feedback Lens

Self Review	Technology Coordinator & STEM Teacher Feedback Lens A—ample evidence; P—progressing (some evidence); ? —not evident yet	Principal Review
	establishes a positive rapport with students, parents, staff and the public	
	teaches robotics and drones, coding, podcasting, web design, yearbook design, and film production	
	stays up to date on current technology supports for learning	
	supports staff with technology needs (Smartboard, projectors, Google Docs)	
	coordinates technology workshops to enhance staff use of technology with students	
	recommends and implements school systems software	
	updates the school website	
	manages general email accounts for staff	
	arranges for telecommunication or technology repairs	
	ensures smooth operation of equipment (computers, etc.)	
	maintains and manages telecommunications network for staff and administration (class phones and console operation)	
	responds to school leaders immediately during working hours and within 24 hours	
	supervises during designated lunch or recess duty	
	completes weekly log of work tasks	

Comments: (documented in email or document attached to email after a discussion of at least two areas of strengths and two areas for improvement).

of the ratee," adding "most of what is being measured by the ratings is the unique rating tendencies of the rater."[2] Thus, ratings reveal more about the rater than they do about the ratee.

Like the gradeless option for students, such options can exist for school employees. If the system and tools used to guide employees toward the mission of the organization is one that is trusted, then it is possible that the tools themselves can be part and parcel of a quality professional growth experience.

Action Items

Ask school administrators if they can pause, start, or study the following:

- *Pause* the use of job descriptions that do not define a detailed scope of work.
- *Pause* disconnects between job descriptions, feedback, goal setting, and growth plans.

Table 10.2: Sample Receptionist and Data Coordinator Feedback Lens

Self-Assess	*Receptionist & Data Coordinator Feedback Lens* *A—ample evidence; P—progressing (some evidence);? – not evident yet*	Supervisor Review
	provides data management support for the school leadership team	
	implements a smooth system for administering statements, collections, and populating information in databases	
	prepares admission packages (details of process; application forms; links to family handbook)	
	develops and manages a check list for the registration process to ensure accurate completion of process	
	maintains confidentiality with respect to all data entries	
	provides daily office and receptionist support	
	coordinates data entry in admission database for all new and returning students	
	works with school leaders to ensure smooth admissions and re-enrollment process	
	manages and maintains annual immunization forms as required for each student	
	ensures all required admission documents are in digital files	
	updates and maintains back-up copies of all databases on a regular basis	
	ensures exit family documents are communicated in a timely manner	
	receives and reviews application contents for accuracy and completion	
	sends receipts of application and enrollment confirmation letters in a timely manner	
	follows up immediately to ensure all data in application is complete	
	ensures careful attention to detail	
	maintains student records according to provincial/state standards	
	maintains secure access and data submissions to the government database	
	makes lists of individuals authorized for student pickup	
	manages payments to vendors and purchases	
	assists in purchase of book orders, new equipment/art materials	
	returns communications from families within 24 hours; if away, forwards all communications to a pre-designated school leader	
	provides positive uplifting experience for families, staff, and vendor contacts	
	completes weekly log of work tasks	

Comments: (documented in email or document attached to email after a discussion of at least two areas of strengths and two areas for improvement).

- *Pause/reduce* the number of subjective qualifiers (adequate, satisfactory, good, very good, excellent, outstanding, exceptional) to give a clearer picture for improvement.
- *Start* ensuring quality ongoing professional feedback and performance review processes for non-instructional staff in school.
- *Start* considering the creation of hybrid jobs that may mix various responsibilities and possibly teaching roles, if employees are qualified.
- *Start* providing funds for non-instructional staff to take part in workshops or conferences.
- *Study* survey data to gain insight into job-related stakeholder perceptions.
- *Study* current research on quality performance reviews in schools and institutions/businesses outside the field of education.
- *Study* or review trends and a range of ways school systems operate (i.e., https://www.microschoolrevolution.com/founder-article/establishing-your-microschool/; https://www.forbes.com/sites/mikemcshane/2021/03/02/so-you-want-to-start-a-microschool/; https://www.tampabay.com/archive/2012/10/24/non-instructional-staff-grows-faster-than-student-population-new-study-shows/).

What do you think schools need to pause, start, or study about assessing non-instructional staff?

NOTES

1. Murphy, N. (April 29, 2019), https://www.strategicpay.co.nz/News/x_post/Why-a-job-description-shapes-a-performance-review-00162.html.

2. London, M. (2001), 170.

11

Who Assesses the Watch Dogs?
Why If?

WHAT IF TRUSTEES OR BOARD MEMBERS TOOK PART IN RIGOROUS PERFORMANCE REVIEWS?

If you are a school trustee reading this introduction, you must wonder where this chapter is headed. Beyond media pressure or voting elected trustees in or out of office, how are school governing officers held accountable for their actions, or non-actions? Trustees might be referred to as the "watch dogs" who provide oversight over schools. Ideally, their role would not be one that intimidates other community members, but one that is supportive in nature. In the case of all public and nonprofit institutions, trustees have the responsibility to make sure that the school leadership is effective, and funds are not misappropriated.

According to the Oregon School Boards Association: "Lack of leadership is a frequently discussed topic in many school districts." They added: "The first indicator of a problem is thinking that one's election to the school board qualifies one to lead. The second symptom is *believing* that one's election to the school board qualifies one to lead."[1]

In a perfect world school trustees would have at least a few education courses in their experience portfolios. Their role yields enormous responsibility. A strong Board of Trustees or Governors should represent a cross-section of different skill sets; however, they are not often encouraged to use them, beyond giving their advice.

It is often cited in school trustee handbooks that these elected or appointed officials should be "hands off," in terms of contributing actual work for the school or district. For instance, one school may have a lawyer on board willing to draw up sample agreements for hiring purposes, or a professional fundraiser who is eager to be a key player in a campaign, but often these folks simply weigh in on what others are hired to do. While schools should not overburden volunteers, it could be an incredible cost savings for schools to utilize the talent sets of their trustees more.

The question often arises as to whether these directors or governors should play a more active role in the leadership of a school. Would a trustee, who volunteers to listen to students read their writing, or work with a team of coders, really be disruptive? Probably not, but this line of thinking rubs against the grain of the accepted practice of keeping school trustees at arm's length. These key leaders need to be welcomed into the field because they are the forces who make budget and priority decisions.

It could be argued that trustees need to understand the context of teaching and learning in order to make informed decisions about it, so schools not only need to consider letting them in, they would need to figure out a way to ensure they learn more about the field of education.

Ideally, the best trustees take courses in education, enroll in quality Harvard Project Zero-type[2] workshops, and engage in dialogue about innovative teaching and learning practices. How can they ever find out about current educational research and "outlier" ideas for improving schools if they rely only on their own experience, and the patterns of former trustees?

Trustees could benefit from being a part of professional development and strategic planning that is informed by ideas that can shape innovation, not simply rollover to make a dated system more efficient.

Trustees need to look beyond simple data dashboards and what floats at the surface of issues. What makes a great school does not fit on a single data page. When such folks at the top of the education food chain can realize this, then educational cultures will be ready for constructive systematic change. A new way of viewing trustee work harnesses the capacity of all stakeholders to build or support genuine trust.

Regrettably, there are some examples of ill-intended political folks who take on the trustee role searching for what's not working, so it is understandable that educational insiders tend to protect their turf. Likewise, there are some trustees who do not trust the people in their organizations. Rather than let the worst scenarios guide the role description, perhaps there is an alternative path that can be generated, one that is based on collegial, collaborative trust.

An incredible team of trustees in Middleburg, Virginia, took on the enormous task of founding a new school. When the doors opened each morning, the Board chair and the school principal greeted each family as they dropped off their kids for school. This lead team shared powerful and supportive chats daily between the opening and closing bell. They developed a trusting relationship, aware that their actions were fiercely focused on how to build an ideal school.

The small board was made up of equally caring people, including the mayor. One board member was instrumental in coordinating the school gardens, and another member helped design the school safety plan. How could a school leader refuse the expertise of someone who worked for the CIA! Another trustee had been deeply involved in the film industry as a Bollywood actress and film maker. She volunteered to teach a class in movie making. These trustees modelled volunteerism on an extraordinary level. Schools can benefit from the diverse talents of strong trustees.

Further research into cases of active trustee involvement in community schools might provide more valuable insight into the possibilities of such a seemingly untapped resource pool. Schools tend to operate within a culture that accepts trustees on a drive-by basis. That is, drop in, shake hands, but do not get too comfortable, as this might disrupt the day. Schools can continue to keep trustees on leashes and perpetuate a *Groundhog Day*-type existence, or they can consider expanding their roles to be more active and connected to the life of the school.

Quality schools can be led by proactive governance teams that can do much more than respond to crises. So how should trustees or Board of Directors be assessed? Public schools are often reviewed by state, provincial, or national authorities that do not focus attention on the actual school boards.

Independent and charter schools, however, usually are accredited by an agency or association such as the Middle States Association (MSA),[3] National Association of Independent Schools (NAIS),[4] International Baccalaureate (IB),[5] Canadian Accredited Independent Schools (CAIS),[6] and the Independent School Management (ISM).[7] Their standards serve as criteria for assessing the quality of how the Board behaves as a whole.

According to CAIS, effective governance is "critical to the long-term success of Independent Schools." They added that good governance can "steward and safeguard the health of their Schools for future generations" and ensure "the School has a clear strategic direction, provides appropriate risk oversight," and that the School "has leadership capacity and resources and effectively manages Board performance."[8]

Quality professional accreditation groups such as CAIS include descriptions of specific indicators for each standard, so Board members can have a clear understanding of their responsibilities. Trustees at the public, independent, and charter school level have significant responsibilities, and given they control the budget, their education and understanding of schools should be paramount. How often do trustees take part in professional development activities? How often do they participate in education conferences? Too often the governance role is a reactionary or political one, but imagine what could happen if trustees were expected to be more proactive?

Action Items

Ask trustees if they pause, start, or study the following:

- *Pause* elevated weighting of standardized test scores as *the* measure of a school's strength.
- *Pause* using limited data on dashboards for decision-making purposes.
- *Pause* doing the same things and expecting different results.
- *Start* using multiple talents to support school and administrative teams.
- *Start* learning about the value of mastery-based reporting practices.
- *Start* recognizing the value of portfolio work.
- *Start* paying attention to the value of extracurricular, volunteer, and internship experiences.
- *Study* governance guides and take part in professional growth activities.
- *Study* various accreditation standards.
- *Study* (Follow/Read) educational books, articles, and websites (i.e., MindShift).

What do you think stakeholders need to pause, start, or study to address trustee accountability?

NOTES

1. https://www.osba.org/Resources/Article/Board_Operations/Is_Your_School_Board_Dysfunctional.aspx.
2. http://www.pz.harvard.edu.
3. https://www.msa-cess.org.
4. https://www.nais.org.
5. https://www.ibo.org.
6. https://www.cais.ca.
7. https://isminc.com.
8. https://www.cais.ca/accreditation/accreditation-overview/2021-cais-national-standards.

12

Goodwill Hunting

What If?

WHAT IF PHILANTHROPISTS BECOME MORE AWARE OF PEER-REVIEWED RESEARCH IN EDUCATION?

Many stakeholders in public, independent, and charter schools have benefitted from generous philanthropic donations. Fundraising efforts can support the development and further renovations of physical plants, the hiring of planning staff, the professional development of teachers, technology, and other resources, and the reduction in leasing or real estate costs, to name a few.

Start-up funds usually have specific strings attached. Even though experts were well aware that having a successful high school was dependent on a strong team of feeder elementary schools, it was difficult to stretch the scope of funding for a new charter school in Detroit to open its doors prior to ninth grade. Funding requirements can guide, but at the same time limit the potential for school success.

Many accountability expectations from funders for charter schools require high test scores in order to sustain funding. Often gaps in learning are so widespread that even characters from the Marvel comics cannot make up for the lost learning overnight. Philanthropists often assume that a turnaround in scores can happen within a school year.

Too often, foundations representing generous donors require ongoing testing data as *the* measure of growth. The sense of urgency is grounded in good intentions; however, the immediate reassurance in the form of narrow test scores can actually do more damage than good in the long run.

Unfortunately, it takes time, upwards of three to five years, to build an industrious and high-achieving culture. A mismatch is evident between the needs of the funders and capacity of a culture to magically produce results.

In fact, the amount of practice testing and overvaluing of testing functions as a deterrent to improvement. Philanthropists and the people they trust to manage their foundations need to be more aware of educational research and, consequently, what is doable in schools in short and longer time frames.

The Walton Foundation,[1] for instance, was pitched for funding from a vibrant, enthusiastic and passionate founding team eager to build an ideal school. They presented an inspiring list of qualitative objectives for the committee to consider. It was surprising, however, how much the grant committee focused on the plan to increase test scores, as if this metric was a litmus test for a great school. In their view, this would be the evidence that their investment in the school was worthy of consideration.

Given that the school was new, the founding team wanted to be realistic, not knowing the learning histories of the 120 students who would come to the school from 30 or more different elementary schools. On the one hand, the founding school team wanted to build an empowering learning culture with abundant evidence of qualitative growth; on the other hand, they did not want to over-promise quantitative gains. The founders were committed to designing and implementing a school with a sustainable and dynamic learning culture. In the end, the decision-makers rejected their request for funds.

It is possible that if this funding decision team had a deeper understanding and expertise in education, that this school might have been the recipient of this philanthropic gift. One cannot assume that the folks administering funds would have a background in educational research. Educational experts would know it can take upwards of three years for schools to achieve high scores on standardized tests. Just as schools need to improve, so too should the tools used to assess the quality of a funding application.

The Blackbird Foundation presented an impressive philanthropic effort as it supports "young, passionate wild hearts working on creative projects in Australia or New Zealand." Mini-grants in the amount of $1,000 were awarded based on three criteria: creativity, conviction, and inspiration. The following refreshing set of questions were established to help guide funding start-ups:

- How does your work showcase your originality, whether that be conventionally or not?
- How are you exploring your curiosities and passion?
- How have you shown commitment to this passion?
- How have you built prototypes of your machine?
- Have you interviewed subjects for your podcast?
- Are you inspiring others to be creative along the way?
- Can you build and share in public to empower others?
- Will others follow in your footsteps?[2]

It is reasonable to expect results in a timely manner. However, knowing what it takes to make a sustainable difference means that patience is required, as well as time to review many reliable kinds of evidence of growth and success. In addition to making donations each year to charities, the Paterson-Smith Family Foundation[3] dedicates funds to support various efforts in the community, and beyond. The funders take time to read in depth about what the applicants plan to do and place significant trust in causes deemed worthy of short- or long-term support.

The foundation began by supporting Kids, Cops and Computers/COMKids, a program[4] that outfitted kids who were at-risk of not finishing high school with laptops and home access to the Internet. The compelling string attached was that these students had to become e-pals with police officers. After several decades of support, this charity has helped hundreds of college-bound and graduating students. The impact took time to take shape but was worthy of the wait.

Here is the rub. There are so many great causes, but so little time to read about them all. It is easy to be inundated with requests for donations. There are too many websites and newsletters to keep track of, and often not enough time to verify the integrity of the agencies. The lack of time and often interest in reading the fine print can make philanthropists vulnerable to manipulation. In education, many generous people have been disappointed in their investments, and therefore hesitant to make future donations.

The cost of building and operating a school is a significant investment of time and money. Educators alone spend an incredible amount of time dedicated to their profession outside the typical school day. While long hours may be assumed to be part of the job, it can tax the energy of these professionals significantly. If everyone expects quality teaching, then new school structures need to be considered and designed, so that time, beyond an hour a day, is built in not only for preparation, but ongoing development. Serious systematic changes require more funds, but also a will to repurpose existing funds.

It is so easy for philanthropists to get lost in a tsunami of white papers and policy documents on education. There is always one more article you can read to feel prepared for philanthropic decision-making. Such materials are often penned at the school district level, state or provincial department of education level, and more recently a trend coming from associations, agencies, and universities. The in-box can be constantly stretched to download a hundred and more page manuscripts.

To make sound decisions, it is important that funders understand as much as possible about the educational contexts being supported. It's not enough to grasp the executive summary shared by various charitable causes; to be effective, philanthropists need to be aware of what's happening in the field. What other goodwill agencies are competing for donors? What, if any, disputes or objections exist that run counter to the missions of the charities? How much money is dedicated to overhead?

Donors need to think carefully about what schools to support, which students to support, and what causes would truly make a difference in the lives of young people. Educational philanthropists are busy people. It is rare if they have time to go back to school and learn about peer-reviewed research in education. Yet, their donated dollars can often be wasted if they do not have a solid grasp of what innovations are worthy of supporting, and which ones may not be in the best interest of all students. The bottom line is that donors do not technically have to be accountable to anyone, yet their funds can be so influential.

In a more ethical sense, it makes sense that philanthropists, or their representatives, should not be disconnected from rigorous educational research. Philanthropists can do more than trust people who need funding. What if Bill Gates, Warren Buffett, or Sam Walton had time to learn about more effective evidence of success in schools? Armed with understandings, surely their goodwill could have more widespread impact.

Philanthropists need some assurance that their well-earned dollars will be put to good use. Two things are for sure: Assuming that great schools can be defined on a single-page dashboard doesn't cut it, nor can significant achievement scores emerge overnight. Philanthropists need to roll up their sleeves and know much more about the context of education before judging gains based on narrow quantitative norms.

Some may say that affluent people are too busy or do not know better, but they didn't acquire their wealth by trusting the numbers on a few viewgraphs. Given the need for funding to support innovation and school improvement, it makes sense to begin the conversation about the viability and credibility of generating quality assessment tools that can improve philanthropic choices, too.

Action Items

Ask philanthropists if they pause, start, or study the following:

- *Pause* the elevated weighting of test scores as *the* measure of a school's strength.
- *Pause* using limited data on dashboards for decision-making purposes.
- *Pause* doing the same things and expecting different results.
- *Start* learning about the value of mastery learning and reporting practices.
- *Start* asking questions about the costs of administrative overhead.

- *Start* asking questions about the volunteer work of the Board of Directors.
- *Study* (Follow) MindShift (https://www.facebook.com/MindShift.KQED/); https://milkeninstitute.org/article/how-evaluate-returns-philanthropic-investment.
- *Study* and take courses/workshops in education in order to have a big picture understanding of how peer-reviewed research should inform quality school practices.

What do you think grant distributors need to pause, start, or study?

NOTES

1. https://www.waltonfamilyfoundation.org/grants.
2. https://blackbird.foundation.
3. https://torontofoundation.ca/meet-our-philanthropists/.
4. https://comkids.ca.

13

School Assessment Whisperers
What If?

WHAT IF SCHOOLS TAKE PART IN QUALITY ACCREDITATION AND RIGOROUS REVIEW AT ALL LEVELS?

After considering alternative ways of assessing students, staff, trustees, and funders, how can schools be assessed more effectively? Some real estate agents may find lists of schools ranked via standardized tests as a simple way to identify the "best schools," but such a narrow analysis and communication to potential home purchasers can be misleading.

There is much to review when making a call about a quality school. With the current volume of documents that should be reviewed in determining quality schools, it is no surprise that novices might turn to the results of high stakes testing as an oversimplified litmus test of a school's merit.

Stakeholders need to be more aware that accountability of a complex school organization cannot be drilled down to a data chart. Schools need new systems of accountability that inspire more students to master learning. The majority of young people should not feel swallowed up by unrealistic and unfair assessment processes that run rampant over their dreams. What students do in school needs to focus on the skills and understandings they require to be successful in life, not in the past, but in a foreseeable future. Being highly proficient on standardized tests is not a predictor of future success.

We need to hold schools accountable for gaining more insight into the depth of learning. The obituary is an invitation, not an account of one's life; by attending a funeral or memorial, you learn about life stories, much more than a dashboard of numbers. When talking with people, one discovers the depth of what they know. At the end of the day, a life is much than a "one-pager."'

Similarly, when hiring teachers, it's important to view the depth of their experiences. How refreshing it would be to welcome a "new-age" resume that spills over to the second or third page. Limiting the volume of material in a resume makes it easier to breeze through a load of them, but much like the automatic car wash misses the detailing, so too do one-pagers.

To find and cultivate an ideal school, it begins with the selection of incredible teachers that usually have amassed powerful experiences that move the word count beyond the single page. School leaders must take time to make these choices, pay attention to portfolios, watch potential candidates teach a sample class, and let the interview spill beyond 30 minutes. In the long run, rushed "hires" can be much more damaging to tolerate as mediocre team players than doing the rigorous work up front.

In much the same vein, colleges need to hire more experts to do their admission vetting. Relying on SAT or ACT scores may seem like an easy way out, but it's not the best way to select good fits for a school. It should not be about convenience, or that nuisance phase: "It's the best we can do!"

Many independent schools and some private schools take part in various accreditation processes. One review experience requires teams of teacher-leaders from other schools to read a self-study collated from the school under review. This introduction to the school happens through the self-study read, in advance of taking part in a multiple-day site visit, depending on the size of the school. The team members seek to answer two questions:

- Is the school doing what it says it is doing?
- Is what the school is doing meeting quality standards?

After the visit, reviewers typically write a report with suggestions, recommendations, commendations, and either an endorsement of the accreditation, or not. Such a process can be viewed as a powerful accountability measure on several fronts. First of all, members of the school team must do a serious self-reflection about their school that includes an explanation of areas that need improvement. Staff members then need to articulate their strengths and challenges to an independent professional reviewer team. Finally, schools need to plan and act on the recommendations in the final accreditation report.

Some reputable school accreditation agencies include: Middle States Association (MSA), The National Association of Independent Schools (NAIS), The Canadian Accredited Independent Schools (CAIS), Advanced Education, and Independent School Management (ISM).

Public school districts do not participate in accreditation led by external agencies, unless the schools are required to meet additional standards, such as the International Baccalaureate (IB). Public schools build in their own internal reviews, and in some jurisdictions they participate in state or provincial level reviews that involve more documentation and less in-school time visitations, if any. In the case of public charter schools in the United States, most officials pay attention to attendance, re-enrollment, test scores, and the growth trends in test scores.

In DC, the charter schools were required to go through an external accreditation process, as well as a qualitative review process conducted by the single authorizer in the community. Such reviews that involved on-site visits duplicated the accreditation process, and in some cases the feedback was contradictory. Identifying the most credible reviewers is key to ensuring an integral process.

At one school, initial visits from the Middle States Association team members gave the school positive feedback according to their set standards, but the DC Charter Board reviewers documented contrary views. In this case, the problem with the authorizing entity writing a review is that it can be tainted by the test scores themselves. There would be a serious disconnect if a qualitative site review indicated a school was demonstrating quality practices, if the same school yielded lower test scores.

Standardized test scores should not influence a qualitative site review. It would be in the best interest of those looking to ratify the test scores to align the qualitative site reviews with the weaker results. It doesn't make sense for an authorizing entity to duplicate review efforts; data gathered from independent accreditation reviews would be a more responsible and less biased practice.

Furthermore, the DC Charter Board site review team used four quality parameters: "distinguished," "proficient," "basic," and "unsatisfactory," increasing the degree of subjectivity. There was no research about how such categories evolved, were field tested, or further documented in white papers.

With no evidence that different reviewers would assign the same scores, especially for "basic" and "proficient" categories, such a process and findings should be open to challenge. External accreditors with no agendas could simply provide feedback to document strengths, suggestions, and recommendations for improvement based on standards that align with informed practices grounded in peer-reviewed research.

Accreditation reviews use a three-tiered system for providing feedback. Schools may receive recommendations, suggestions, or recognition for exceptional or distinguished practice, based on rigorous set standards in key areas such as school culture, academics, leadership, mission, human resources, facilities, governance, and finances. Suggestions are not required, but recommendations need to be addressed within a timeline in order for schools to maintain their accreditation. A team of respected educators from other schools review extensive school documentation in advance of visiting the school for several days.

If the team determines that the school under review is not adhering to a specific standard, they make specific recommendations, whereby the school usually has within a year to provide evidence of the change. Some schools can receive upwards of 30 to 50 recommendations in a review; a quality review process is like a serious comprehensive case study that involves both the writing of an internal report by the school in advance of the visit and an extensive qualitative external response by the review team.

Schools expect outside reviewers to share recommendations, and together with their own internal reviews shape the groundwork for a school improvement plan. It makes sense that schools engage in an accreditation review in three to five year cycles, which can complement their strategic planning. All schools can truly benefit from independent reviews.

An external review is only as good as the quality of the people conducting the activity. The expertise of accreditation teams is often underrated, but the potential for such expertise has much to offer in terms of strategic planning and directing school improvement initiatives. What can be missing from the design of review teams are university experts and researchers. These voices can share updates on current research and informed practices, as well as contribute suggestions and recommendations for improving and updating of the accreditation standards themselves.

Some schools outsource a review process to private consulting firms, who can find it profitable to identify problems. In some cases, school audits may recommend themselves as "turnaround" fixers, equating school improvement to a renovation project, as if preparing a property for up-sale. Such reviews do not seem to warrant the building of trusting commitments for sustainable growth. Beware the helpers promising dashboard gains, and be sure to check the time the leaders of such organizations have actually been in classrooms. Quality reviews should not be written based on 10-minute quickie visits.

It's important to think about who should profit from the recommendations of a quality review. Schools should be wary of the reviewers that specify what products to buy, who to hire, or what services they can provide to champion the change. It is important to research the long-term sustainable impact of outside consultants. How long do they stay in a school or a community? How much did they pocket, and did they succeed in making school improvements?

The reputable consultants, agencies, and associations make sure their budgets (and line items) are clear and transparent. When anyone professes to be the good guys, ask to see their budgets. Be sure they are not simply good at lining their own pockets.

As much as it is valuable to take part in a school review conducted by reputable professionals, it is important that accreditation groups and authorizers also take part in rigorous reviews of their services. The quality of such work should also be addressed by those responsible for the operations of such reviews. In some cases, it is the mayor, the governor, the premier, or other political figures; these representatives will need to be held accountable for the inner workings of the reviewing process, especially if they are at the receiving end of public funds.

Given there is a common problem of student engagement, it makes sense that reviewers will make practical recommendations for schools to address these issues. The cupboards in education are not bare. It's not all doom and gloom. Researchers for decades have filled the shelves with solid findings that support classroom engagement for many more students than the current institutions will allow.

It is important for school reviews to pay close attention to the kinds of assessment that students and staff must endure. Who said fun and testing had to be mutually exclusive? Schools can be happy places. Joy should not exist as a sporadic thread; joy can be a catalyst for learning! Schools can be very effective at weaving together fun within the learning mix. Joyful experiences can be like glue for cultivating teacher and student relationships, fundamental building blocks for powerful learning cultures.

A quality school review would focus significant attention on school climate. One memorable review included the documentation of evidence of school culture. Once a year, at one school, teachers took on phantom names (i.e., insects, superheroes) to participate in a fun lunchtime Teacher Torture Week. Staff members would compete to emerge as the hula hoop, blind jello-eating, or egg toss champion. Students would sponsor a phantom name in advance (pennies dedicated for local charities), and then cheer them on with roars of laughter during the events. The pseudonyms helped to level the teacher popularity playing field.

Silly games can promote a positive school culture. How many people remember the student-staff baseball game at the end of the school year? At another school in Virginia, the community participated in "Sport Fan Day," every Wednesday. Comfy shoes and sport jerseys were the norm; even wearing a Maple Leaf hockey sweater while knee-deep in a sea of Washington Capital fans was tolerated!

At a performing arts school in Washington, DC, in the middle of a professional development week, the staff, organized in Broadway show teams, took part in an impromptu ping pong blowing relay that sprung up around the outside of the lunchroom. The speed at which staff were slithering along the ground blowing these ping pong balls was indeed the stuff of memory building. Laughter rebounding from the walls can be so infectious. Being silly helped form some precious bonds and memories.

You can't really put such experiences into a quantitative dashboard, yet they matter when it comes to engagement. Joyful experiences can enhance school cultures, and positive environments can cultivate student engagement. It's not fun when the focus is on a narrow view of achieving top test scores that is won by a single school. It's not fun to work in a place where stakeholders are not happy.

In 2014, Willis noted in her article "Neuroscience Reveals that Boredom Hurts": " . . . the standards set for student mastery now require students to digest an excessive volume of information. These have spawned corresponding increases in direct instruction and memorization requirements—stressors that increase boredom and damage the brain."[1] Such is the antithesis of fun.

When more members of the student body are underachievers or perform poorly, it is difficult to feel the joy of school. When status is only afforded to a ranking function of assessment, you technically have one "winner" and a few near the top who are happy. Wiggins (2015) clearly points out that authentic assessment minimizes "needless, unfair, and demoralizing comparisons of students to one another."[2] A majority of the players often feel like "losers" resigned to the lower rungs of the ranking ladder.

It won't matter how many Teacher Torture Weeks, Sports Fan Days, or ping pong blowing relays happen if more students do not succeed academically. So, what can be trusted to guide schools toward a new assessment path? For starters, educators need to assess students and staff in more inspiring and engaging ways. School leaders need to encourage action research at the school level so educators can gather feedback from students about what is engaging and what is not. School systems need to have experts adjudicate a fair and inspiring school accreditation process.

Stakeholders can all promise to ask those in positions of responsibility how they are delivering on their engagement promises. There is no need to whisper sweet nothings; schools need to roar about the need to bring credible assessment into the fold, the kind that enables joy and oozes reputable research-based accountability practices. There are too many hiding places that hush the inner workings of schools. The public is often recipients of profuse verbose documents, filled with so many details that it requires a backhoe to remove the weeds that cloud the clarity and purpose of schooling.

With so much attention paid to obese policies and documents, void of executive summaries, it is easy for schools to keep on doing what they are currently doing without any disruption. Gaps can hide in massive volumes of data. How can we find the needle or source of a problem if we keep enlarging the haystack? By padding documents with extraneous material, school systems can continue to snow the people who pay for them.

What is screened from public consumption is the fact that the popular factory model of schooling makes it difficult to implement best practices. While experts do need to explain better what these ingredients are, it is necessary to assure people that progressive education ideas have been vetted and scrutinized through the "holy grail" of peer-reviewed research.

It's not enough to hear whispers for assessment reform; schools need to find a way to transform more teachers, students, parents, trustees, and philanthropists into becoming ambassadors and quality assessment whisperers, moved to promoting more effective feedback reform in all schools.

When it comes to assessing the quality of a school, educators need more surprises—good surprises, the kind that lead us to creative new solutions. Having quality school reviews can provide some fresh directions and encouragement to make more surprises in education a reality.

Action Items

Ask educators within various school systems if they pause, start, or study the following:

- *Pause* using limited data on dashboards for decision-making purposes.
- *Pause* doing the same things and expecting different results.
- *Start* cultivating joy in schools in explicit ways.
- *Start* using accreditation experts with independent reviewers.
- *Start* gathering more student, teacher, and parent satisfaction surveys to inform strategic and school improvement planning.
- *Start* providing time for teachers to plan for ideal practice.
- *Start* using mastery learning and reporting practices.
- *Start* ensuring that the physical plant contributed to learning.
- *Start* being more transparent about school budgets.
- *Study* (Follow) MindShift (https://www.facebook.com/MindShift.KQED/).
- *Study* and pilot action research to discover new ways to advance learning and assessment.

What do you think schools need to pause, start, or study to address school improvement?

NOTES

1. Willis, J. (2014), https://kappanonline.org/neuroscience-reveals-that-boredom-hurts-willis/.

2. Wiggins, G. (2015), https://www.teachthought.com/pedagogy/authentic-assessment/.

14

The Sound of Silence

What If?

WHAT IF DECISION-MAKERS PAID ATTENTION TO STUDENT VOICES?

Paying attention to student voices might shine a light on many things schools need to change. Darkness can simmer in the sacred halls of schools when there is a lack of clarity and opportunity for quality communication. Schools publish lengthy documents, enroll too many students, and build physical plants so complicated and large that it's impossible to keep track of bodies in the building, emotionally, socially, and intellectually. Our future world assets (students) become test scores and enrollment data, all squished together on a single page dashboard, a truncated version of what matters in a school culture.

The larger the school, the more staff to supervise, and the more students who can fall through the cracks. Stakeholders should worry about schools going through the motion, drifting in and out of sameness. As the lyrics of Simon and Garfunkel (S & G) so poignantly message: "People talking without speaking; People hearing without listening; In restless dreams, I walk alone. No one dared disturb the sound of silence."

Many educators know well the warnings to stand back and not disrupt the status quo. People are often put in positions where they are expected to weigh the collateral consequences of transparency. The withholding of information paves the way for short-sighted decision-making. Bystanders can be quite adept at echoing the "sounds of silence." As S & G echoed: "Silence like a cancer grows . . ."

How often do schools go about making our day-to-day decisions based on partial information—or are they confident that we have a good sense of the full story? In our busy world, even when comprehensive reporting is transparent, it can be so easy to hide details in the thick descriptions of audits, studies, and white papers. Educators often rely on abridged news articles, executive summaries, and quick poll results to capture a glimpse of a story.

In school, progressive educators pride themselves on their capacity to teach students how to inquire, think critically, and read between the lines. Yet, it is difficult for many students to apply these skills when given too many lines to read and too many assignments to complete. The more educators load on the volume of text, the easier it is to be lost in the verbiage.

What grows in the future assessment starships in schools does not have to be hidden or be beyond the reach of all community members. Systems that perpetuate "bigness" in terms of expanding the number of students, staff, families, size of the physical plant, and the number of digits in a budget simply feed the chaos that contributes to the cloaking of learning. The more schools a Board must manage, the easier it is to operate under the radar and simply address abbreviated data that shortcuts a true image of schooling.

Schools tend not to be soft places. Let's face it. There are plenty of words that are used to describe the personal and social intentions on websites, in hallways, and in all sorts of handbooks and mission statements. The actions, however, that deliver warmth, empathy, and a sense of community in schools are quite rare.

It does not take many schooled years before students see their classes as a bunch of lame subjects, day in and day out, fueling a "go fetch" phenomenon. If researchers had audio tapes of dining room table conversations for the past century, they might have some compelling data that points to the conclusion that school, at least many parts of it, is boring. To the question "What did you learn in school today?", a critical mass of young people return a blank stare.

There are plenty of sweet documents singing the praises of standardized achievement; at the same time stacks of books and blogs exist, spouting the bitter tastes and faces of failed schools. For many, the school circulatory system is moving to the beat of a boring testing drum. By now most educators have seen the graph that reveals the results of the 2014 Gallup poll of 5th through 12th grade students with respect to feeling engaged, or not, in school.

Eighty percent of elementary students indicated they were attentive in class; by the time students were in high school, this score fell to 40%.[1] With an *n* of close to a million students, McLeod's findings from the 2016 study shows a similar decline to the 2013 Gallup numbers.[2] Can educators honestly say that most students love coming to school?

Many educators have viewed graphs and tables that reveal declining levels of engagement, but what are people doing about it? And what about the increases in occurrence of anxiety and suicide at alarming rates? If schools are places where kids spend a significant amount of time, then schools need to be places that address these serious health issues. Is it possible that school and, more specifically, assessment practices are contributing to these health crises among young people?

Unlike canines who bring you their leash to rush to their dog parks, many students are not eager to go on this walk to be in school. Zachary Jason wrote about students being "bored out of their minds." When presented with a list of 14 objectives on a Gallup Poll in 2004, "bored" was chosen most often, by half the students." He added: "Only 2 percent said they were never bored. The evidence suggests that, on a daily basis, the vast majority of teenagers seriously contemplate banging their heads against their desks."[3]

PISA conducted international research in 2000 among OECD countries on the sense of belonging and participation in school, as possible indicators of engagement. They found:

- about 25% of all students were considered to have a low sense of belonging
- about 20% were regularly absent from school

And they concluded that students who attend schools with a concentration of students from low socioeconomic families were more likely to be disaffected by school.[4]

Mehta and Fine (2017) acknowledged that many students have six or seven 45- and 50-minute classes each day, which is often spent reviewing homework and doing menial tasks, "exacerbating boredom." Referring to extra-curricular programs, they claimed: "there is much to be learned from extra-curricular experiences." And that if the "extras became the rule and not the exception, perhaps students would be as excited for what happens during the school day as they are for what happens after the final bell.[5]

On a similar theme, the executive editor of *EdWeek* noted that "kids are right. School is boring" as the number 1 of 10 big ideas school leaders must tackle. He added: "The most meaningful learning happens outside school."[6] Schools need to explore what engagement looks like in out-of-school experiences, so they can make engagement happen inside. For starters, schools that support inquiry and project-based learning (PBL) curriculum have made meaningful strides in reducing boredom. According to Mehta and Fine (2017), there are fewer bored students in PBL schools.[7]

Cater, Machtmes, and Fox (2013) noted that youth "understood that they were respected because their opinions were solicited and adults listened. Youth knew that adults were listening because they wrote down their ideas and continued to ask them to share ideas."[8] Adding that "the more trust that youth have in themselves, the adult leaders, and their peers, the more willing they are to engage in the decision-making process." Student engagement should matter in curriculum design.

Students should do things in school that matter to themselves and others. What they do can be more about meaning-making than memorizing. No longer should boredom be collateral damage of a mediocre education. How many more studies need to be conducted about student engagement? How many ways can students say they are bored before decision-makers will respond? The sounds of silence can mute equitable action; no longer should student voices and needs be muffled by the roar of flames protecting sameness.

Action Items

Ask educators within various schooled systems if they can pause, start, or study the following:

- *Pause* doing the same things and expecting different results.
- *Start* cultivating curriculum that encourages creativity and original thought in explicit ways.
- *Study* much more about curriculum, teaching, and learning and its connection to quality assessment.

Ask more parents to:

- *Start* participating in parent education opportunities to expand their world view of what teaching and learning can be.
- *Study* more research-informed options for engaging student learning.

What do you think schools need to pause, start, or study to increase awareness of assessment?

NOTES

1. https://news.gallup.com/opinion/gallup/170525/school-cliff-student-engagement-drops-school-year.aspx.
2. Doxtdator, B. (February 5, 2017), https://www.longviewoneducation.org/the-politics-of-engagement-from-school-to-work/.
3. Zachary, J. (Winter 2017), https://www.gse.harvard.edu/news/ed/17/01/bored-out-their-minds.
4. https://www.oecd.org/education/school/programmeforinternationalstudentassessmentpisa/33689437.pdf.

5. Mehta, J. & Fine, S. (2017), https://www.gse.harvard.edu/news/ed/17/01/why-periphery-often-more-powerful-core.

6. Bushweller, K. (January 8, 2019), https://www.edweek.org/teaching-learning/the-kids-are-right-school-is-boring/2019/01.

7. Ibid.

8. Cater, M., Machtmes, K., & Fox, J.E. (2013), 10, http://www.nova.edu/ssss/QR/QR18/cater31.pdf.

15

Forging New Paths for School Assessment

The OECD (2013) acknowledged that the simple knowledge test can be "well-suited to assess the outcomes of traditional teaching approaches based on rote learning and knowledge transfer." However, they also claimed "that such tests are less adequate when it comes to assessing complex competencies."[1] The world grows increasingly complex every day. Preparing students to thrive in the 21st century and learn a curriculum that embraces the 22nd century requires much more than a transmission approach to teaching and learning.

"Coherent assessment frameworks," according to the OECD (2013), "should aim to align curriculum, teaching and assessment around key learning goals and include a range of different assessment approaches and formats, along with opportunities for capacity building at all levels."[2] What if the public insisted on assessment accountability as much as they focus on teacher, student, and school accountability?

When young people begin their formal education, many proceed to be trained, not necessarily educated. The educated mind can think critically and solve problems beyond the scope of a standardized test, so schools need to do something about updating systems that place unwarranted emphasis on testing. It's time to strike out the testing team at bat.

The worshipping of testing as the core of education is flawed, and it's not funny what's happening in many North American schools today:

- It's not funny that some kids achieve mastery and others do not.
- It's not funny that more young people are avoiding educational careers.
- It's not funny that schools are being shut down based on quantitative data rankings.
- It's not funny that so many kids are unhappy, have anxiety, and are thinking about suicide.

Most stakeholders have not only survived school, but many have thrived in spite of a narrow focus on standardized testing; students, past and present, have figured out how to roll over and complete the tasks required to achieve various diplomas, certifications, or degrees. Educators have earned their worker bee badges of honor! Stakeholders have become so accustomed to the routine of testing that they rarely question their instincts or think there might be other ways of designing schools to be more efficient, cost effective, and engaging. Stakeholders assume all students are happy; forgetting, like the pain of labor, that not every test leads to an easy and heartfelt delivery.

Even though some learning institutions appear to be the product of elegant precision, stakeholders need to ask: "Do these tests and performance reviews simply polish the same old school machine?" You might be thinking: "Education can't be that bad"; "It's moving in a good direction"; "All we need to do is to keep doing what we're doing, just execute better." No matter how much one polishes the system, the critical mass of engaged and inspired cultures will remain less than ideal.

Dated models of assessment require a full scale-change. Mindsets of parents, voters, and those in the thick of things making educational decisions need to stop turning their backs on what the peer-reviewed research has been saying for decades. A major shift—not to the left or right,but a full-on revolution of the systems that handcuffs young learners and frustrated teachers to dated and boring ways of doing school—is needed.

If the general population is not made aware of the opportunities to improve assessment, the overall state of schools will not improve. The current system is pushed along by people who accept a factory model of education. If stakeholders all agree that we are no longer in the industrial age, why are so many schools wagged by the assessment tail of the dog that emulates learning as some paint-by-numbers exercise? It is time to step aside and admit many schools have disappointed too many people. Enough, already. School does not have to be boring!

Parents and teachers can ask schools to provide education seminars or professional development about standards-based grading, competency-based education, test fatigue, project-based learning, critical and creative thinking, multi-age learning, internships and experiential learning (locally and abroad), and social and emotional development. No one needs another workshop on examining quantitative data. What's the point of churning data that perpetuates a dated system?

Imagine if all students experienced progressive report cards that clarified exactly what has been mastered? Imagine if teachers were given preparation time to generate their own assessment rubrics, aligned with their teaching? Imagine if schools provided semesters where students worked as apprentices outside the school? Imagine if schools offered micro-credentials in technology and the trades? Imagine high schools that partner with local colleges to provide opportunities to secure credits in advance of college entry? Imagine how building experiences into school that boost resumes could enhance engagement?

Most North Americans have been to school, but few have a real say in how it works and how it can change. Educators do have choices: They can settle, that is, continue to fuel the school engines of the past or they can design a better way, one that moves beyond the land of numbers. How can nations thrive by rewarding a small fraction of students? To fix the current assessment trajectory that took hundreds of steps to put in place requires at least one hundred more steps to clear a new road for learning, one where more young people can belong and lead successful schooled lives.

Assessment Tools and Systems: Meaningful Feedback Approaches to Promote Critical and Creative Thinking is somewhat of a path of disruption, a wake-up call of sorts, to those who bathe in a forest of assessment apathy. School leaders need to do less talking and take more action about what is not working with assessment in schools. Stakeholders should now be able to ask politicians and government workers in education more targeted and potentially stinging questions. As readers, there are new considerations to ponder. Maybe the dog days of assessment can be over!

This read is a call to action. While it may be possible to better cope with the realities of testing mindsets, stakeholders can vet more assumptions about testing, and if politicians do not heed our cry, we can walk with our feet toward braver leaders, willing to embrace the systemic changes needed in assessment that can fuel a better education for the future.

When new ideas come to a table, people may choose to act on them right away, pause current activity, or study the ideas further. Wherever you land on the continuum, this book should raise some challenging questions about school assessment and feedback. Without informing all stakeholders of outlier ideas, how can schools improve?

Think about what it means to have life experiences. They are much more than a test score and a viewgraph filled with spiffy looking bar charts. Hopefully, this look into school feedback structures can inspire more people to reclaim their own assessment stories and realize that what is of value does not have to fit into a one-page dashboard.

Students, parents, and educators can define school and work lives in different ways. Learners do not have to be defined by positions on a bell curve. Schools do not have to be a shadow of their missions. This book has attempted to strip down the education jargon and hand over some new outlooks, beyond politics, to banter about in school staff rooms, conferences, or holiday dinners. It's not often educators get a chance to poke at assessment tools and systems and, better yet, the places kids are sent to—six hours a day, ten months a year, for more than a decade of their lives.

It would be less work if schools could bask in the reflective breeze of sluggish sameness, but it is not news that things need to change to make schools better places for all students. The system has worked overtime on testing and judging young people, but how well do schools help students think critically and creatively? How well do young people know how to be joyful and how to bring joy to others? Many parents wish their kids had more opportunities to learn to think, reflect, relax, and have fun at school, so now it's time to do something about it.

There is so much more to explore and consider for ongoing and deeper discussions about schools and assessment. Research that is contextual and interdisciplinary should provide more examples of how assessment is used in classrooms and what role language can play in implementing quality assessment.

In a report synthesizing discussions from 35 scholars who met in Mexico in 2002, Candelam, Rockwell, and Coll (2004) noted the need for interdisciplinary research as a focus for future research agendas. To systematically link research, educators need to embrace interdisciplinary study. As noted: "This implies finding ways of embedding detailed analysis of interaction within the larger structures of activities and lessons, and each of these within the institutional and social context, in order to understand their interrelations."[3]

Further attention to how teacher preparation programs can integrate with ongoing induction and professional growth experiences throughout a teacher's career will be a timely focus, given the reduced number of applicants interested in teaching careers.

An expanded look at other areas of assessment not addressed in this text might include a renewed examination of how school systems move students from one grade to another, a deeper dive into multi-age learning and classroom assessment, a comprehensive analysis of peer assessment, a discussion of criteria for issuing high school diplomas, an examination of effective moderation practices, exemplar use and meaningful implementation of metacognitive practices, a review of research on student-designed assessment, and as the identification of computer-based tests that adapt to learners.

This is not the first assessment story, nor will it be the last. If educators truly want to improve education, they must improve assessment. School systems need new options for assessment tools and practices to support young people to thrive, be industrious, and be thoughtful in a future they will be responsible for.

NOTES

1. OECD (2013), 216.
2. Ibid.
3. Candelam, C., Rockwell, E., & Coll, C. (2004), 710.

References

Assessment and its interrelated role in curriculum and the culture of the school is not a topic in education that is going away. More and more educators and researchers are paying serious attention to its influence and quality. At the time this resource was written, these experts played a key role in informing and supporting this work: *Assessment Tools and Systems: Meaningful Feedback Approaches to Promote Critical and Creative Thinking.*

4H Club. https://4-h.org/wp-content/uploads/2016/02/Rural-Youth-Development-Youth-Leading-Community-Change-Evaluation-Toolkit-Color.pdf.

ACT. https://www.act.org.

Adie, L.E, Willis, J., & Van der Kleij, F.M. (February 17, 2018). "Diverse perspectives on student agency in classroom assessment." *Australian Educational Researcher, 45*: 1–12 https://link.springer.com/article/10.1007%2Fs13384-018-0262-2.

Adie, L., Wyatt-Smith, C., & Haynes, M. (April 22, 2020). "On-line moderation of teacher assessment using exemplars." Australian Catholic University. https://www.acu.edu.au/research/our-research-institutes/institute-for-learning-sciences-and-teacher-education/our-research/projects/online-moderation-of-teacher-assessment-using-exemplars.

Allal, L. (2010). "Assessment and the regulation of learning." In Penelope Peterson, Eva Baker, & Barry McGaw (Eds), *International Encyclopedia of Education* 3, pp. 348–352. Geneva, Switzerland: Elsevier. https://unige.ch/fapse/people/allal/doc/Allal2010.pdf.

Allal, L. (2013). Teachers' professional judgement in assessment: A cognitive act and a socially situated practice. *Assessment in Education: Principles, Policy & Practice, 20*, 20–34.

Alphonso, A. (April 21, 2018). Government-commissioned report recommends Ontario should phase out Grade 3 EQAO test. *Globe and Mail.* https://www.theglobeandmail.com/canada/article-government-commissioned-report-recommends-ontario-should-phase-out/.

Altan, S., Lane, J.F., & Dottin, E. (2017). "Using habits of mind, intelligent behaviors, and educational theories to create a conceptual framework for developing effective teaching dispositions." *Journal of Teacher Education,* 1–15. https://

www.habitsofmindinstitute.org/wp-content/uploads/2014/09/Servet-Dottin-HOM-Conceptual-Framework.pdf.

American Educational Research Association, American Psychological Association, & National Council on Measurement in Education (Eds.). (2014). *Standards for Educational and Psychological Testing*. American Educational Research Association.

Armida, G. (March 3, 2019). "Extra credit diminishes everything and everyone." *The Teacher and The Admin*. https://theteacherandtheadmin.com/2019/03/03/extra-credit-diminishes-everything-and-everyone/.

Arter, J., and J. Chappuis. *Creating and Recognizing Quality Rubrics*. Portland, OR: ETS, 2006.

ASCD. https://www.ascd.org.

Atkinson, K. (2012). "Pedagogical narration: What's it all about?" *The Early Childhood Educator*. http://www.jbccs.org/uploads/1/8/6/0/18606224/pedagogical_narration.pdf.

Atkinson, R. C., & Geiser, S. (2009). "Reflections on a century of college admissions tests." *Educational Researcher, 38*, 665–676.

Baker, J. (March 10, 2019). "'On its last legs': Why the world is abandoning NAPLAN-style tests." *Sydney Morning Herald*. https://www.smh.com.au/education/on-its-last-legs-why-the-world-is-abandoning-naplan-style-tests-20190308-p512v4.html.

Baker, E.L., & Linn, R.I. (2004). "Validity issues for accountability systems." *Redesigning Accountability Systems for Education*. New York: Teacher's College Press.

Barendsen, L., Bither, C., Clark, S., Fischman, W., Gardner, H., McHugh, K., & Mucinskas, D. "The Good Project Lesson Plans." Harvard Porject Zero. Harvard Graduate School of Education. https://static1.squarespace.com/static/5c5b569c01232cccdc227b9c/t/60ca3500b0b3ae4fbe941f69/1623864590713/Good+Project+Lesson+Plans+-+fillable.pdf.

Bartlett, K. https://commongroundcollaborative.org.

Berger, R. (April 18, 2017). "Beautiful work." https://my.pblworks.org/resource/document/beautiful_work.

Berkowitcz, J., & Myers, A. (September 7, 2017). "Don't get rid of grades. Change their meaning & consequences." *Education Week*. https://www.edweek.org/leadership/opinion-dont-get-rid-of-grades-change-their-meaning-consequences/2017/09.

Biggs, J., & Tang, C. (2011). *Teaching for Quality Learning at University: What the Student Does*. Berkshire, England: Open University Press. https://cetl.ppu.edu/sites/default/files/publications/-John_Biggs_and_Catherine_Tang-_Teaching_for_Quali-BookFiorg-.pdf.

Black, P., & Wiliam, D. (October, 1998). "Inside the Black Box." *Kappan*.

Blackbird Foundation. https://blackbird.foundation.

Booth, D. (2008). *It's Critical: Classroom Strategies for Deepening and Extending Comprehension*; (2011). *Caught in the Middle: Reading and Writing in the*

Transition Years; (2013). *I've got Something to Say: How Student Voices Inform Our Teaching.*

Borko, H., Liston, D., & Whitcomb, J.A. (January 1, 2007). "Genres of empirical research in teacher education." *Journal of Teacher Education*, 3–11.

Brennan, R.T., Kim, J., Wenz-Gross, M., & Siperstein, G.N. (2001). "The relative equitability of high-stakes testing versus teacher-assigned grades: An analysis of the Massachusetts Comprehensive Assessment System (MCAS)." *Harvard Educational Review, 71*(2), 173–216.

Brookhart, S. M. (1994). "Teachers' grading: Practice and theory." *Applied Measurement in Education, 7*(4), 279–301.

Brookhart, S. *Grading*. Columbus, OH: Pearson Merrill Prentice Hall, 2004.

Brookhart, S.M., Guskey, T. R., Bowers, A.J., McMillan, J.H., Smith, J.K., Smith, L.F., Stevens, M.T., & Welsh, M.E. (December, 2016). "A century of grading research: Meaning and value in the most common educational measure." *Review of Educational Research, 86(*4), 803–848.

Buck Institute. https://www.pblworks.org/why-project-based-learning.

Buckingham, M. (2007). *Go: Put Your Strengths to Work.* https://www.marcusbuckingham.com/defining-strengths/.

Bushweller, K. (January 8, 2019). "The kids are right: School is boring." *Education Week.* https://www.edweek.org/teaching-learning/the-kids-are-right-school-is-boring/2019/01.

Cairns, R. B., Cairns, B. D., & Neckerman, H. J. (1989). "Early school dropout: Configurations and determinants." *Child Development, 60*, 1437–1452.

Campbell, C., Clinton, J., Fullan, M., Hargreaves, A., James, C., & Longboat, K.D. (March 2018). *Ontario: A Learning Province*. Toronto: Ontario Ministry of Education.

Canadian Accredited Independent Schools (CAIS). https://www.cais.ca.

Canadian Accredited Independent Schools (CAIS). https://www.cais.ca/accreditation/accreditation-overview/2021-cais-national-standards.

Canadian Assessment for Learning Network (CAFLN). https://cafln.ca.

Candelam, C., Rockwell, E. & Coll, C. (2004). "What in the world happens in classrooms? Qualitative classroom research. *European Educational Research Journal, 3*(3).

Cater, M., Machtmes K., & Fox, J.E. (2013). "A phenomenological examination of context on adolescent ownership and engagement rationale – Qualitative report." *The Qualitative Report*, 18(Art. 31), 1–13. Retrieved from http://www.nova.edu/ssss/QR/QR18/cater31.pdf.

Clarke, P., Owens, T., and Sutton, R. *Creating Independent Student Learners: A Practical Guide to Assessment for Learning*. Winnipeg, MB: Portage and Main Press, 2006.

Cliffordson, C. (2008). "Differential prediction of study success across academic programs in the Swedish context: The validity of grades and tests as selection instruments for higher education." *Educational Assessment, 13*, 56–75.

ComKids. https://comkids.ca.

Common Core State Standards. http://www.corestandards.org.

Common Ground Collaborative (CGC). https://commongroundcollaborative.org.

Connell, R. (2013). "The neoliberal cascade and education: An essay on the market agenda and its consequences." *Critical Studies in Education, 54*(2), 99–112.

Cooper, D. *Talk About Assessment: Strategies and Tools to Improve Learning.* Toronto, ON: Thomson Nelson, 2007.

Costa, A., & Kallick, B. (2000). *Habits of Mind.* ASC: Alexandra, VA.

Costa, A., & Kallick, B. https://www.habitsofmindinstitute.org/habits-of-mind-dispositions-of-success/.

Council of Chief State School Officers and National Governors Association Center for Best Practices. (2010). *Common core state standards initiative.* Washington: Council of Chief State School Officers & National Governors Association Center for Best Practices. http://www.corestandards.org/the-standards.

Cox, J. (2020). http://www.thoughtco.com.

Coyle, D. (2009). *The Talent Code: Greatness Isn't Born . . . It's Grown. Here's How.* New York: Bantam Books.

Croft, A., Coggshall, J.G., Dolan, M., Powers, E., & Killion, J., (April, 2010), "Job-Embedded Professional Development: What It Is, Who Is Responsible, and How to Get It Done Well. Issue Brief." National Comprehensive Center for Teacher Quality. Washington, DC.

Dadani, S. (2019). The politics of standardized testing in Ontario: Critically assessing the impact on learners, teachers and administrators. A thesis submitted in conformity with the requirements for the degree of Doctor of Education. Department of Social Justice Education University of Toronto. https://tspace.library.utoronto.ca/bitstream/1807/97346/1/Dadani_Sharmin_201911_EdD_thesis.pdf.

Danielson, C. *Framework for Effective Teaching.* danielsongroup.org.

Danielson, C. (2013). *Enhancing Professional Practice: A Framework for Teaching: Teacher Leadership that Strengthens Professional Practice.* Alexandra, VA: ASCD.

Darling-Hammond, L. (2010). *The Flat World and Education*; (2012). *Getting Teacher Evaluation Right: What Really Matters for Effectiveness and Improvement.*

Darling-Hammond, L. (February 17, 2019). "Implications for educational practice of the science of learning and development." *Applied Developmental Science, 24*(2). https://www.tandfonline.com/doi/full/10.1080/10888691.2018.1537791.

Delong, J. (Ed). (2001–2008). *Passion in Professional Practice; Action Research in Grand Erie.* Brantford; Grand Erie District School Board. Retrieved August 20, 2021, from https://www.actionresearch.net/writings/ActionResearch/passion/index.html.

Delong, J. (2021). "Mentoring for Co-Creating Knowledge in Living Educational Theory Cultures of Inquiry. Paper presented at 2021 Action Research Network of the Americas Virtual Conference," June 18, 2021. Retrieved from https://www.actionresearch.net/writings/arna/jddARNA180621.pdf.

Developing Inquiring Communities in Education Project (DICEP). https://www.researchgate.net/publication/227193287_DICEP_Promoting_Collaborative_Inquiry_in_Diverse_Educational_Settings.

Dewey, J. (1899). *The School and Society and the Child and the Curriculum.* University of Chicago Press.

Diamond, P. (1991). *Teacher Education as Transformation: A Psychological Perspective*. Milton Keynes, UK: Open University Press.

Disney Institute. https://www.disneyinstitute.com/about/.

Dixon, C.N., & Green, J. (March, 2009). "How a community of inquiry shapes and is shaped by policies: The Santa Barbara Classroom Discourse Group experience as a telling case." *Language Arts 86*(4). https://www.jstor.org/stable/41483538.

Doxtdator, B. (February 5, 2017). "The politics of engagement from schools to work." *Essays on the Intersection of Politics and Pedagogy*. https://www.longviewoneducation.org/the-politics-of-engagement-from-school-to-work/.

Drake, S. (2012). *Creating Standards Based Integrated Curriculum*. Thousand Oaks, CA: Corwin.

Dweck, C. (2007). *Mindset: The New Psychology of Success*; (2012) *Mindset: How You Can Fulfill Your Potential*. New York: Balantine Books.

Dweck, C. https://www.youtube.com/watch?v=J-swZaKN2Ic; https://www.youtube.com/watch?v=hiiEeMN7vbQ.

Earl, L. (2003). *Assessment As Learning*. Thousand Oaks, CA: Corwin.

EL Education. "Leaders of their own learning: Chapter 5: Student-led conferences." https://eleducation.org/resources/chapter-5-student-led-conferences.

European Council of National Associations of Independent School (NCAIS). https://www.ecnais.org.

Estess, E. http://www.ethanestess.com/statement.html.

Euclid Mathematics Contest. https://www.cemc.uwaterloo.ca/contests/euclid.html.

Ferriter, B. (2021). "Punitive grading policies don't teach kids to act responsibility." *Building Confident Learners*. https://buildingconfidentlearners.com/2021/12/punitive-grading-policies-dont-teach-kids-to-act-responsibly/.

Fullan, M. (2016). *The New Meaning of Educational Change*. New York: Teachers College Press.

Future Learn. https://www.futurelearn.com/programs.

Garcia, E., & Weiss, E. (April 16, 2019). "U.S. schools struggle to hire and retain teachers." Economic Policy Institute. https://www.epi.org/publication/u-s-schools-struggle-to-hire-and-retain-teachers-the-second-report-in-the-perfect-storm-in-the-teacher-labor-market-series/.

Gardner, H. (July 18, 2002). "Test for Aptitude, Not for Speed." *New York Times*. https://www.nytimes.com/2002/07/18/opinion/test-for-aptitude-not-for-speed.html.

Gladwell, Malcolm (2002). *The Tipping Point: How Little Things Can Make a Big Difference*. Boston: Back Bay Books.

Gladwell, M. (2011). *Outliers: The Story of Success*. New York: Little, Brown and Co.

Good, R. (2011). "Formative use of assessment information: It's a process, so let's say what we mean." *Practical Assessment, Research, and Evaluation*, 16(3). https://scholarworks.umass.edu/pare/vol16/iss1/3/?utm_source=scholarworks.umass.edu%2Fpare%2Fvol16%2Fiss1%2F3&utm_medium=PDF&utm_campaign=PDFCoverPages.

Green, J., & Castanheira, M.L. (2012). "Exploring classroom life and student learning: An interactional ethnographic approach" In *Understanding Teaching and*

Learning: Classroom Research Revisited. The Netherlands: Sense Publications. https://www.researchgate.net/publication/286508162_Exploring_Classroom_Life_and_Student_Learning.

Guskey, T. R. (2002). Computerized gradebooks and the myth of objectivity. *The Phi Delta Kappan, 83*(10), 775–780.

Guskey, T.R. (December 2004). "The Communication Challenge of Standards-Based Reporting," *Phi Delta Kappan*: 326–329.

Guskey, T.R. (2009). Grading policies that work against standards . . . And how to fix them. In T.R. Guskey (Ed.), *Practical solutions for serious problems in standards-based grading* (pp. 9–26). Thousand Oaks, CA: Corwin.

Guskey, T.R. (2017). "Don't get rid of grades: Change their meaning and consequences" *EdWeek.* http://tguskey.com/dont-get-rid-grades-change-meaning-consequences/.

Hargis, C.H. (1990). *Grades and grading practices: Obstacles to improving education and helping at-risk students.* Springfield, MA: Charles C. Thomas.

Hargreaves, A., & Fink, D. (2005). *Sustainable Leadership:* with Dennis Shirley (2012). *The Global Fourth Way: The Quest for Educational Excellence.*

Hargreaves, A., & Fullan, M. (2012). *Professional Capital: Transforming Teaching in Every School. Professional Capital: Transforming Teaching in Every School.* New York: Teachers College Press.

Harvard Project Zero. http://www.pz.harvard.edu.

Hattie, J. (June, 2015). *What Works Best in Education: The Politics of Collaborative Expertise.* Pearson. https://www.pearson.com/content/dam/corporate/global/pearson-dot-com/files/hattie/150526_ExpertiseWEB_V1.pdf

Hogan, A., & Williamson, B. (2021). "Provocation 3: The electric 'shock' of the COVID-19 crisis on schooling." In Wyatt-Smith, C., Lingard, B., & Heck, E. *Digital Disruption in Teaching and Testing: Assessments, Big Data, and the Transformation of Schooling.* New York: Routledge.

Holt, J. (1964). *How Children Fail.* New York: Sage.

IBM Design Thinking Badges. https://badges.mybluemix.net/badgedirectory?filter=Design%20Thinking.

Independent School Management (ISM). https://isminc.com.

International Baccalaureate (IBO). https://www.ibo.org.

Jason, Z. (Winter, 2017). "Bored out of their minds." *Harvard Ed. Magazine.* https://www.gse.harvard.edu/news/ed/17/01/bored-out-their-minds.

Joint Health and Safety Committee. https://shop.wsps.ca/pages/jhsc-certification-overview.

Junior Achievement. (2017). "3DE: An Integrated and Comprehensive Partnership Model." https://www.atlantapublicschools.us/cms/lib/GA01000924/Centricity/Domain/11340/3DE%20Resources.pdf.

Khan Academy. https://www.khanacademy.org.

Koh, Y. (August 9, 2021). "How schools are rewriting the rules on class time for students—and even ditching grade levels." *The Wall Street Journal.* https://www.wsj.com/articles/how-schools-are-rewriting-the-rules-on-class-time-for-studentsand-even-ditching-grade-levels-11628517648.

Kohn, A. (June 16, 2019). "Can everyone be excellent?" *New York Times*. https://www.alfiekohn.org/article/excellence/?print=pdf)

Koretz, D. (2017). *The Testing Charade: Pretending to Make Schools Better.* Chicago: The University of Chicago Press.

Laveault, D., & Allal, L. (2016). "Implementing assessment for learning theoretical and practical." In Laveault. D. & Allal, L. (Eds), *Assessment for Learning: Meeting the Challenge of Implementations. The Enabling Power of Assessment 4.* Switzerland: Springer.

Lawrence, M. (2020). *Testing 3,2,1 What Australians can Learn from Finland.* Melbourne Books.

London, M. (2001). *How People Evaluate Others in Organizations.* Mahwah, NJ: Lawrence Erlbaum Associates Publishers.

Lucas, B., & Claxton, G. (August, 2009). "Wider skills for learning." NESTA. https://www.researchgate.net/publication/273454585_Wider_skills_for_Learning?channel=doi&linkId=5502cf3b0cf231de076f9286&showFulltext=true.

Macdonald, R.F. (2004). "Strategies for enquiry and problem-solving." In Macdonald, R.F. & Savin-Baden, M. *A Briefing on Assessment in Problem-based Learning*, LTSN Generic Centre Assessment Series. https://www.plymouth.ac.uk/uploads/production/document/path/2/2434/Assessing_Enquiry_and__Problem_Based_Learning.pdf.

Macdonald, R.F., and Savin-Baden, M. (2004). *A Briefing on Assessment in Problem-based Learning*, LTSN Generic Centre Assessment Series. https://www.plymouth.ac.uk/uploads/production/document/path/2/2434/Assessing_Enquiry_and__Problem_Based_Learning.pdf.

MacMath, S. (December 9, 2021). Email communication.

Maker, Ed. https://makered.org/professional-development/maker-educator-micro-credentials/.

Marshall, K. (January 2, 2014). "Teacher evaluation rubrics." The Marshall Memo. https://www.marshallmemo.com/articles/Teacher%20rubrics%20Jan%202014%20corr.pdf.

Marzano, R. (2006). *Classroom Assessment & Grading that Works.* Alexander, VA: ASCD.

Marzano, R., Frontier, T., & Livingston, D. (2011). *Effective Supervision: Supporting the Art and Science of Teaching.* Alexander, VA: ASCD.

Masterclass. https://www.masterclass.com

McCrea, B. (Spring, 2019)."Levelling up your accounting and finance credentials." *Insight Magazine.* https://www.icpas.org/information/copy-desk/insight/article/spring-2019/leveling-up-your-accounting-and-finance-credentials.

McGraw-Hill. https://www.mheducation.com/news-media/press-releases/mcgraw-hill-offers-simnet-credentialing-program-to-college-students.html.

Mehta, J., & Fine, S. (2017). "Why the periphery is often more powerful than the core," *Harvard Ed. Magazine.* https://www.gse.harvard.edu/news/ed/17/01/why-periphery-often-more-powerful-core

Microschool Revolution. https://www.microschoolrevolution.com/founder-article/establishing-your-microschool/.

Middle States Association (MSA). http://middlestates.org/index.html?modified=284.
Milken Institute. https://milkeninstitute.org/article/how-evaluate-returns-philanthropic-investment
Mindshift. https://www.facebook.com/MindShift.KQED/.
Model United Nations. https://www.un.org/en/mun/model-un-guide.
Moreton, J. (April 2021). "Sugata Mitra: PhD-style vivas should replace exams." *Tes Magazine.* https://www.tes.com/magazine/teaching-learning/secondary/sugata-mitra-phd-style-vivas-should-replace-exams.
Murphy, N. (April 29, 2019). "Strategic pay and strategy for non-profits." https://www.strategicpay.co.nz/News/x_post/Why-a-job-description-shapes-a-performance-review-00162.html.
National Association of Independent Schools (NAIS). https://www.nais.org.
Nichols, S. L., & Berliner, D. C. (2007). *Collateral Damage: How High Stakes Testing Corrupts America's Schools.* Cambridge, MA: Harvard Education Press.
Nietzel, M.Y. (November 19, 2021). "University of California reaches final decision: No more standardized admission testing." *Forbes Magazine.* https://www.forbes.com/sites/michaeltnietzel/2021/11/19/university-of-california-reaches-final-decision-no-more-standardized-admission-testing/?sh=450518e2ec58.
Nobel Peace Prize. https://www.nobelprize.org.
O'Connor, K. (1995). *How to Grade for Learning: Linking Grades to Standards*, Second Edition. Thousand Oaks, CA: Corwin.
O'Connor, K. (1999; 2002). *The Mindful School: How to Grade for Learning.* Arlington Heights, IL: Skylight.
O'Connor, K. (January, 2001). "The principal's role in report card grading." *NASSP Bulletin.*
O'Connor, K. (2002). *How to Grade for Learning: Linking Grades to Standards* (2nd ed.). Arlington Heights: Skylight.
O'Connor, K. (2017). "A case for standards-based grading and reporting." *School Administrator.* https://my.aasa.org/AASA/Resources/SAMag/2017/Jan17/OConnor.aspx.
Ontario Institute for Studies in Education (OISE), University of Toronto. https://cpl.oise.utoronto.ca/program_certificate/principals-qualification-program/.
Ontario Ministry of Education. (2010). *Growing Success.* http://www.edu.gov.on.ca/eng/policyfunding/growsuccess.pdf.
Ontario School Board Association (OSBA). https://www.osba.org/Resources/Article/Board_Operations/Is_Your_School_Board_Dysfunctional.aspx.
Ontario Secondary School Literacy Test. http://osslt.eqao.com/scores.html.
Ontario Tech University. https://ontariotechu.ca/microcredentials/what-are-microcredentials/index.php.
Oregon School Boards Association. https://www.osba.org/Resources/Article/Board_Operations/Is_Your_School_Board_Dysfunctional.aspx.
Organization for Economic Co-operation and Development (OECD). (2013). "Student assessment: Putting the learner at the centre." In *Synergies for Better Learning: An International Perspective on Evaluation and Assessment. Paris, France:* OECD Publishing. https://doi.org/10.1787/9789264190658-7-en.

Organization for Economic Co-operation and Development (OECD). (2018). *Preparing our Youth for an Inclusive and Sustainable World: The OECD PISA Global Competence Framework*. Paris, FR: OECD. https://www.oecd.org/education/school/programmeforinternationalstudentassessmentpisa/33689437.pdf.

Outer Limits. https://en.wikipedia.org/wiki/The_Outer_Limits_(1963_TV_series).

Outlier.org. https://www.outlier.org.

Outschool. https://outschool.com/classes/.

Patterson, W. (April, 2003). "Breaking out of our boxes." *Phi Delta Kappan*.

Perkins, S. C., Finegood, E. D., & Swain, J. E. (2013). "Poverty and language development: Roles of parenting and stress." *Innovations in Clinical Neuroscience, 10*(4), 10. https://www.ncbi.nlm.nih.gov/pmc/articles/PMC3659033/.

Pink, D.H. (2012). *Drive: The Surprising Truth About What Motivates Us*. New York: Riverhead Books.

Pink Time. https://www.pinktime.org/about.

Polikoff, M.S., Porter, A.C., & Smithson, J. (2011). "How well aligned are state assessments of student achievement with state content standards?" *American Educational Research Journal, 48*, 965–995.

Poorthuis, A.M.G., Juvonen, J., Thomaes, S., Denissen, J.J.A., de Castro, B.O., van Aken, M.A.G. (August, 2015). "Do grades shape students' school engagement?: The psychological consequences of report card grades at the beginning of secondary school." *Journal of Educational Psychology, 107*(3), 842–854.

Programme for International Student Assessment (PISA). https://www.oecd.org/pisa/.Progress in International Reading Literacy Study (IRLS). https://nces.ed.gov/surveys/pirls/.

Puglisi, J., Machtmes, K., & Green, J. (2013). *The River Project*. https://sites.google.com/rioschools.org/river-literacy-project/home/about?authuser=0.

Reeves, D.B. (December, 2000). "Standards are not enough: Essential transformations for school success." *NASSP Bulletin*.

Reeves, D.B. (December, 2004). "The case against the zero." *Phi Delta Kappan*, 324–325.

Reeves, D. B. (December 13, 2021). "When making the grade takes on new meaning." EdSource. https://edsource.org/2021/when-making-the-grade-takes-on-new-meaning/664591.

Rethinkingschools.org. https://rethinkingschools.org.Rhodes Scholarship. https://www.rhodeshouse.ox.ac.uk/office-of-the-american-secretary/.

Robinson, K. (2009). *The Element: How Finding Your Passion Changes Everything*. New York: Penguin Books.

Robinson, K. (2015). *Creative Schools: The Grassroots Revolution that's Transforming Education*. New York: Penguin Books.

Rumberger, R. W. (1987). "High school dropouts: A review of issues and evidence." *Review of Educational Research, 57*, 101–121.

Ryerson University. https://www.ryerson.ca.

Sahlberg, P. (2011). *Finnish Lessons: What Can the World Learn From Educational Change in Finland?* New York: Teachers College Press.

Sahlberg, P. *Reimagine Schools*. https://podcasts.apple.com/gb/podcast/finnish-lessons-with-dr-pasi-sahlberg/id1397680693?i=1000492848675.

Santa Barbara Classroom Discourse Group. https://www.jstor.org/stable/41483538.

Scholastic Aptitude Test (SAT). https://collegereadiness.collegeboard.org/sat.

Schwartz, K. (February 15, 2017). "Can micro-credentials create more meaningful professional development for teachers?" KQED. https://www.kqed.org/mindshift/47476/can-micro-credentials-create-meaningful-professional-development-for-teachers.

Schwartz, K. (November 15, 2018). "A grading strategy that puts the focus on learning from mistakes." KQED. https://www.kqed.org/mindshift/52456/a-grading-strategy-that-puts-the-focus-on-learning-from-mistakes.

Sellar, S. (2021) "Provocation #5: The COVID-19 pandemic creates opportunities to repair the infrastructure of public schools." In Wyatt-Smith, C., Lingard, B., & Heck, E. *Digital Disruption in Teaching and Testing: Assessments, Big Data, and the Transformation of Schooling*. New York: Routledge.

Selwyn, N. (2021). "Lenses on COVID-19 provocations." In Wyatt-Smith, C., Lingard, B. & Heck, E. *Digital Disruption in Teaching and Testing: Assessments, Big Data, and the Transformation of Schooling*. New York: Routledge.

Shirley, D. (July 5, 2021). "Standardized testing is not the way forward." *CommonWealth Magazine*. https://commonwealthmagazine.org/opinion/standardized-testing-is-not-the-way-forward/.

Spear, T. (2019). *Education Re-imagined: The Schools Our Children Need*. Eaglecliff Publishing.

Spencer Foundation Grant. https://www.spencer.org.

Stiggins. R. (September, 2004). "New assessment beliefs for a new school mission." *Phi Delta Kappan. 86(*1); 22–27. https://journals.sagepub.com/doi/10.1177/003172170408600106.

Stiggins, R.J. (2008). *Student-involved Assessment for Learning* (5th ed.). Upper Saddle River: Merrill, Prentice Hall.

Stiggins, R., & Chappuis, J. (June 24, 2010). "Using student-involved classroom assessment to close achievement gaps." *Theory into Practice,* 11–18. 10.1207/s15430421tip4401_3.

Strauss, V. (March 4, 2019). "'If all of that testing had been improving us, we would have been the highest-achieving nation in the world.' Here's what does work in school reform." *Washington Post*. https://www.washingtonpost.com/education/2019/03/04/if-all-that-testing-had-been-improving-us-we-would-have-been-highest-achieving-nation-world-heres-what-does-work-school-reform/.

Sutton, R. (1995). *Assessment for Learning*. Salford, UK: RS Publications.

Sutton, R. (1991). *Assessment: A Framework for Teachers.* London, UK: Routledge.

Swan, G. M., Guskey, Thomas R., & Jung, Lee Ann. (2014). "Parents' and teachers' perceptions of standards-based and traditional report cards." *Educational Assessment, Evaluation and Accountability*, 26(3), 289–299.

Tassone, M. (November 21, 2021). "A failure at 6? Data-driven assessment isn't helping young children's learning." *The Conversation*. https://theconversation

.com/a-failure-at-6-data-driven-assessment-isnt-helping-young-childrens-learning-169463.

The Wing Institute. https://www.winginstitute.org.

Thoughtco. https://www.thoughtco.com.

Tienken, C. H. (2008). "Rankings of international achievement test performance and economic strength: Correlation or conjecture?" *International Journal of Education Policy and Leadership, 3*(3), 1–12.

Tienken, C. (2013). https://christienken.com/wp-content/uploads/2013/01/PISA_ProblemsAASA.pdf.

Toronto Foundation. https://torontofoundation.ca.

Trends in International Mathematics and Science Study (TIMSS). https://nces.ed.gov/timss/.

Troutman McCrann, J.R. (February 1, 2018). "Putting assessment back in the hands of teachers." ASCD. https://www.ascd.org/el/articles/putting-assessment-back-in-the-hands-of-teachers.

Twilight Zone. https://en.wikipedia.org/wiki/A_Stop_at_Willoughby.

Vasquez, A. (December 19, 2021). "The future of grading: When failure is not an option." *EdSource.* https://edsource.org/2021/when-making-the-grade-takes-on-new-meaning/664591.

Vygotsky, L. (1978). *Mind in Society.* (1934/1964). London: MIT Press.

Vygotsky, L. (1986). *Thought and Language.* London: MIT Press.

Wagner, T. (2015). *Creating innovators: The Making of Young People Who Will Change the World.* New York: Scribner.

Walton Foundation. https://www.waltonfamilyfoundation.org.

Wan, T. (2020, April 7). "Traffic is booming for online education providers. But so are costs." *EdSurge.* https://www.edsurge.com/news/2020-04-07-traffic-is-booming-for-online-education-providers-but-so-are-costs.

Wells, G. (1999). *Dialogic Inquiry: Towards a Socio-cultural Practice and Theory of Education.* Cambridge University Press.

Weston, D. (November 16, 2018). "6 reasons to say no to EQAO." *The Heart and Art of Teaching and Learning.* https://heartandart.ca/?p=7004.

Whitehead, J. (March 9, 2009). "Generating living theory and understanding in action research." *Action Research.* University of Bath. https://journals.sagepub.com/doi/abs/10.1177/1476750308099599.

Wiggins, G. (2015). "27 characteristics of authentic assessment." *Teach Thought.* https://www.teachthought.com/pedagogy/authentic-assessment/.

Wiggins, G., & McTighe, J. (2005). *Understanding By Design,* (2nd Expanded edition). Alexandria, VA: Assn. for Supervision & Curriculum Development.

Wechsler Intelligence Test. https://www.child-psychologist.com.au/wechsler-intelligence-scale-for-children.html.

Wiliam, D., & Leahy, S. (2014). "Sustaining formative assessment with teacher learning communities." Learning Science: Dylan Wiliam Center. https://www.dylanwiliamcenter.com/wp-content/uploads/sites/3/2020/10/DW02-01-Chapter-X-TLC-Paper-03-05-17-Digital.pdf.

Willis, J. (2014). "Neuroscience reveals that boredom hurts." *Phi Delta Kappan.*

Woodcock-Johnson Test. https://riversideinsights.com/woodcock_johnson_iv.

Wormeli, R. (2006). *Fair Isn't Always Equal: Assessing and Grading in the Differentiated Classroom*. Portland, ME: Stenhouse.

Wyatt-Smith, C., & Adie, L. (2021). "The development of students' evaluative expertise: Enabling conditions for integrating criteria into pedagogic practice." *Journal of Curriculum Studies*, *53(*4), 399–419. https://doi.org/10.1080/00220272.2019.1624831.

Wyatt-Smith, C., Lingard, B., & Heck, E. (2020). *Digital Disruption in Teaching and Testing: Assessments, Big Data, and the Transformation of Schooling*. New York: Routledge.

www.ingramcontent.com/pod-product-compliance
Lightning Source LLC
Chambersburg PA
CBHW021843220426
43663CB00005B/383